THE SAMARITAN WAY

Lifestyle Compassion Ministry

DAVID W. CROCKER

To: Nenette,
In appreciation of your
work in using Inasmuch
at Carson-Newman,

David Crocker
Mt. 25:40

CHALICE
CHALICE
P R E S S

ST. LOUIS, MISSOURI

The Columbia Partnership Leadership Series
from Chalice Press

Christ-Centered Coaching: 7 Benefits for Ministry Leaders
Jane Creswell

Coaching for Christian Leaders: A Practical Guide
Linda J. Miller and Chad W. Hall

Courageous Church Leadership: Conversations with Effective Practitioners
John P. Chandler

Enduring Connections: Creating a Preschool and Children's Ministry
Janice Haywood

Every Congregation Needs a Little Conflict
George W. Bullard Jr.

From the Outside In: Connecting to the Community Around You
Ronald W. Johnson

The Heart of the Matter: Changing the World God's Way
Charles Halley

Operation Inasmuch: Mobilizing Believers beyond the Walls of the Church
David W. Crocker

Pursuing the Full Kingdom Potential of Your Congregation
George W. Bullard Jr.

*Reaching People under 40 while Keeping People over 60:
Being Church to All Generations*
Edward H. Hammett with James R. Pierce

Recreating the Church: Leadership for the Postmodern Age
Richard L. Hamm

Renew Your Congregation: Healing the Sick, Raising the Dead
Willliam T. McConnell

Seeds for the Future: Growing Organic Leaders for Living Churches
Robert D. Dale

Spiritual Leadership in a Secular Age: Building Bridges Instead of Barriers
Edward H. Hammett

www.chalicepress.com
www.thecolumbiapartnership.org

This book is dedicated to:

My children, Andy and Emily,
who are constant sources
of pride to me
and whose faithful and sensitive encouragement as I
step out in faith to launch the Ministry I lead
I will always remember as voices as from God
in troubled times.

Cover image: GettyImages and FotoSearch
Cover and interior design: Elizabeth Wright

Visit Chalice Press on the World Wide Web at
www.chalicepress.com

10 9 8 7 6 5 4 3 2 1   08   09   10   11   12   13

Library of Congress Cataloging-in-Publication Data

Crocker, David W.
The Samaritan way : lifestyle compassion ministry / by David Crocker.
    p. cm.
ISBN 978-0-8272-3469-7
    1. Compassion–Religious aspects–Christianity. 2. Church work. 3. Christian life. I. Title.
BV4647.S9C76 2008
241'.677–dc22   2008023011

Printed in United States of America

Contents

Editor's Foreword   viii

Introduction: A Humbled Police Officer   1

1. A Grander Vision   7
   A Better Paycheck
   Wheels and Deals
   Friendship as a Ministry
   Beyond Lifestyle
   The Next Level

2. The Samaritan Way   25
   The Story Still Speaks
   The Story
   Negative Models
   Priorities
   Lessons from a Compassionate Stranger
   Go and Do Likewise

3. It's Not about Us   45
   It's Not Supposed to Be about Us
   We Have Seen the Enemy, and They Are Us
   God's Mirrors
   A Poignant Parable

4. It's about Them   60
   Victims of Homelessness
   Victims of Poverty
   Victims of Disease
   Prisoners
   Not Just Them

5. We Need the Poor   82
   Serving Jesus
   Aware of Human Need
   Purpose for Life
   Spiritual Growth
   Beggars Looking for Beggars

6. Turn Your Chairs Around   100
        A New Reformation
        It's a Big World
        Reworking Evangelism
        Missional Churches

7. Moving Down the Funnel   116
        The Funnel
        Tips for Making Compassion Ministry Part of Your DNA
        The Decision
        Prayer
        Vision

8. Churches That Make a Difference   135
        What Is Church Culture?
        A Culture of Compassion Ministry
        A Tale of Two Churches
        Lessons Learned
        Becoming

Editor's Foreword

Inspiration and Wisdom for Twenty-First-Century Christian Leaders

You have chosen wisely in deciding to study and learn from a book published in **The Columbia Partnership Leadership Series** with Chalice Press. We publish for

- Congregational leaders who desire to serve with greater faithfulness, effectiveness, and innovation.
- Christian ministers who seek to pursue and sustain excellence in ministry service.
- Members of congregations who desire to reach their full kingdom potential.
- Christian leaders who desire to use a coach approach in their ministry.
- Denominational and parachurch leaders who want to come alongside affiliated congregations in a servant leadership role.
- Consultants and coaches who desire to increase their learning concerning the congregations and Christian leaders they serve.

The Columbia Partnership Leadership Series is an inspiration- and wisdom-sharing vehicle of The Columbia Partnership, a community of Christian leaders who are seeking to transform the capacity of the North American Protestant church to pursue and sustain vital Christ-centered ministry. You can connect with us at www.TheColumbiaPartnership.org.

Primarily serving congregations, denominations, educational institutions, leadership development programs, and parachurch organizations, the Partnership also seeks to connect with individuals, businesses, and other organizations seeking a Christ-centered spiritual focus.

We welcome your comments on these books, and we welcome your suggestions for new subject areas and authors we ought to consider.

George W. Bullard Jr., Senior Editor
GBullard@TheColumbiaPartnership.org

The Columbia Partnership,
332 Valley Springs Road, Columbia, SC 29223-6934
Voice: 803.622.0923, www.TheColumbiaPartnership.org

INTRODUCTION

A Humbled Police Officer

A police officer sees the uglier sides of people—domestic violence, crime, and just plain unseemly behavior. Every day or night on the job is different and presents its own challenges. On one particular, snowy night in a Colorado town, an officer of the law was brought face to face with a challenge not so much to his professional competence or strength but to his own values.

Traffic was unusually bad because of the amount of snow. From accident to accident, the officer felt the stress building...and became a little more hardened with each call of an inconvenienced and sometimes foolish driver. Call after call, the hours quickly passed. There was no time to eat. Finally, a break in the calls opened a small window for a quick bite. A local sandwich shop would meet his needs.

While the officer was waiting for his sandwich, another call came in, but this time it was about a hazard in traffic. Having no time to finish his sandwich, he grabbed it and took it with him. He would have to eat it later. The officer was sent to the area of the local homeless shelter. A homeless man in a wheelchair was stuck in the middle of the street. His wheel chair was unable to move in the thick snow. As he approached the area, it became eerily peaceful. The snow was falling gently and only a few cars were out. In the beam of his lights, the officer could see the silhouette of a man in a wheelchair. He was wrapped in blankets, and had on layers of hats, scarves, and jackets. The officer positioned his patrol car so as to protect himself and the man from being struck by oncoming traffic. As he exited his vehicle, he couldn't help but think, "What am I supposed to do?" He knew the shelter was already full for the night. At this time of year they held a daily lottery for the few warm beds the shelter had available.

"Hi, how are you doing?" asked the officer. Expecting to hear curse words and complaints, he was surprised at the man's almost jovial response. He even laughed at his own predicament. It seemed that the concave area of the gutter had become completely iced over, and the wheels of his chair just spun in place.

"I don't have a foot," said the man. The officer asked him where he was trying to go. "Oh, I have a place right over there in the gravel fields." He pointed towards a vacant lot a few hundred yards away. "If you could just give me a little push, I'll be on my way."

The officer looked at the man's chair, which was also a makeshift trailer for his worldly possessions. The officer grabbed the back of the chair and began pushing. This would be hard enough, but given that there was about six inches of snow on the road it was much worse. As they slowly made their way towards the gravel fields, the homeless man talked with the officer, never once whining or complaining about the conditions or the inconveniences these conditions caused him. The man's positive nature and personality shamed the officer for the negative feelings he had been having. The officer had felt put out because he had to stand out in the cold for several minutes at a time while taking care of other people's problems. This man would be sleeping outside tonight.

The man directed the officer to the area where he lived, just a few mounds covered in snow. The man was proud of his "home," even commenting that he needed to pick up the place a bit. It wasn't everyday he had company. They were out of sight from the nearest road, at least to the passersby who would never look in this direction. Travelers were more concerned with keeping their nice cars on the road and getting home to their fireplaces.

"Are you going to be okay here?" asked the officer. "Oh yes," the man responded confidently. "I'll be plenty warm as soon as I crawl under my tarps." The officer learned that this had been the man's home for over two years. He had learned to adapt, having been through plenty of days of bad weather.

The officer wished him luck, and walked away. A lump formed in his throat.

How strange. Nothing had ever made him feel this way in all his duties. He had seen tragedies, gruesome scenes, and had dealt with hundreds of homeless people. Why now? Why this man?

As he trudged through the snow back to his car, he began hearing his pastor's voice in his head. He was recalling the message the previous Sunday. It was about "sharing your lunch," and how Jesus had fed five thousand people one day when a little boy offered what he had.

The officer quickly wrote off that thought. "I can't save everybody." Once back in his car, he had time to pull into a nearby parking lot and finally eat his sandwich. It had been nearly eight hours since his last meal, and he was starving. Each bite of the sandwich only served as a reminder of his selfishness and the thought of a man who was cold, wet, and most definitely hungry.

Again, the pastor's words came into his mind. He thought about how often people avoid doing anything to help people in need because they think, "It's not my problem." Whose problem was this? What could be done to make things better? It became evident that he needed to do something…no matter how small. The officer had not made it a practice of giving to homeless people. He knew that often they used the money to support their addictions. In the five years he had been working the street, he had never given anything to a homeless person.

Back to the sandwich shop he went. For only a couple of dollars, he got a hot sandwich. The clerk smirked at him. "Still hungry?" he joked. "It's for a friend," the officer replied. He took the sandwich and drove toward the man's camp. Doubts crept into his head. Was this patronizing to the man? Would he even be hungry? Did he like this type of sandwich? Was he allergic to wheat? All his thoughts attempted to sway his decision. The officer turned into the gravel lot. There was no turning back.

The headlights of his car lit up the little camp. There was movement under a tarp, and it appeared the man was hunkering down for the night. The humbled officer approached the man, sandwich in hand. "Would you be interested in something to eat?" The man tore the tarps off his head so fast that it startled the officer. His eyes were *huge,* and he was smiling. "Thank you, thank you so much." The man grabbed the bag and prepared to "feast."

The two shared conversation for a few minutes. The officer felt compelled to share in the reason for his return. The man told a bit about his life, that he had been a priest just a few years before. He explained that his wife's death from cancer had been too much for him to bear, and it had driven him to this point. The two connected in a way that was beyond normal or routine duties. It wasn't inappropriate; it was true care and compassion.

As the officer walked away, the man shouted, "God bless!" The officer didn't feel as if he had changed the man's life. He was sure there was so much more he could have done. But this wasn't about the act itself. The lessons learned from the homeless man were so much more valuable than the pocket change he had spent on the sandwich. The officer knew that this experience was more for himself than for the homeless man. This was a gift from God.

The lessons learned? What could be more inconvenient than having to crawl through six inches of snow to find a warm place under a tarp to sleep? What things in life were really worth complaining about? What do we take for granted? Do our attitudes truly reflect our appreciation for everything God has given us? The officer knew all too well that his answers seemed quite embarrassing when compared to the attitude displayed and the adversity his homeless friend lived with daily.

How much this officer received, just for simply being willing to share his lunch![1]

What do you feel when you read this story? If you're like me, something inside you warms up. You may even get a lump in your throat or shed a tear. In many ways this story of "on the way" mercy is like many others. But no matter how many times we hear or read them, they move us.

A couple of things are happening here. First, this is a story about a man doing the right thing in the right way. Something about that inspires us and draws us in. We can't resist. Such a story penetrates the hard shell of indifference some of us have worked hard to construct for protection.

Second, compassion–I mean *true* compassion, spontaneous, unrequited mercy without regard for reward–is irresistible. No matter how busy or sophisticated or powerless we are, we know the world abounds with needs. We also know that when we learn of someone who has responded to just one of those needs in genuine compassion, we are moved and we are not likely to forget it. Unfortunately, this is a commentary on the hardness of our world as much as it is an acknowledgment of authentic mercy when we encounter it.

This book is meant both to alleviate some of the hardness of the world and to help more people become like this policeman. It is written to help followers of Jesus everywhere discover lifestyle compassion ministry. I have spent the last twelve years doing what I could to mobilize believers beyond the walls of their churches. It was a dozen years ago that a church I was serving as pastor developed the highly effective model of community ministry known as "Operation Inasmuch"–a one-day, hands-on blitz of believers into their community, conducting a wide range of compassion ministry projects helping people in need. I did this while ministering as a full-time pastor in good-sized congregations. At the beginning of 2007, I stepped out of the pastorate to serve as the Executive Director of Operation Inasmuch, Inc., an independent, nonprofit ministry that acquaints congregational leaders with the Operation Inasmuch model and trains them to conduct the event.

Soon after launching this full-time ministry, God convicted me that my goal for the ministry was inadequate. God is not satisfied with seeing churches mobilized for a day or two of compassion ministry each year. *God wants to see all believers involved in this kind of ministry as a lifestyle!* The New Testament makes this clear. Jesus modeled it and called his followers to do it. Compassion ministry is not an add-on to the Christian life, an option only for those who tend to be more fanatical. It is inherent in what it means to follow Jesus. It is an essential part of discipleship, every bit as essential as prayer, worship, Bible study, Christian fellowship, evangelism, and giving.

God's Spirit has led me to write and publish *The Samaritan Way*. It follows on the heels of my first book–*Operation Inasmuch:*

Mobilizing Believers beyond the Walls of the Church–as if to say, "Okay, you've done the one-day thing. Now let's move on to a *lifestyle* of compassion ministry."

The book will share many stories like the one at the beginning of this section. It's obvious where the book gets its title, but this title is more than a reference to one of the best-known stories of all time; it is also an indication of the role of story in this book. God has and continues to work through persons such as the policeman who helped the wheelchair-bound, homeless man. Furthermore, God uses the stories of these "Samaritans" to move us all where he wants us to be.

Chapter 1 recounts the story of four friends who have transitioned into lifestyle compassion ministry toward the grander vision of discipleship Jesus gave. Chapter 2 celebrates the powerful lessons of Jesus' story of the Good Samaritan. That wonderfully inspiring story contains everything we need to know about lifestyle compassion ministry. Chapter 3 exposes the inward focus of the church as a major hindrance to lifestyle compassion ministry. Chapter 4 examines the plight of people in need. Only when we understand and truly see their needs will we ever respond as we ought. Chapter 5 suggests that the poor fill a need for followers of Jesus. Got your attention? Check it out.

There is a fresh movement of God in churches and individual believers. Chapter 6 reviews some of the remarkable Kingdom events God is bringing about. This is nothing less than a new reformation of the church, and compassion ministry is at the heart of it. As with my first book, I am committed to giving my readers practical ways to implement a lifestyle of compassion ministry. Chapter 7 provides a step-by-step process individuals and congregations may use to move in this direction. Chapter 8 shares the stories of churches I know that have cultivated a culture of compassion ministry; it has actually become part of their DNA!

Notes

[1]Unpublished story by Jeremy Frenzen, officer in the Longmont, Colo., Police Department, shared with and edited by the author.

1

A Grander Vision

When [Jesus] finished speaking, he said to Simon, "Put out into deep water, and let down the nets for a catch."

Simon answered, "Master, we've worked hard all night and haven't caught anything. But because you say so, I will let down the nets." (Lk. 5:4–5)

They didn't see it coming. They had no way of knowing how much their lives would change that day. They were just common fishermen, ordinary men who put in long hours on their boats fighting the elements. The limits of their knowledge and tools eked out a living from the sometimes generous, sometimes grudging, sea.

They didn't see it coming–Jesus using their boat as a pulpit for one of his famous teaching sessions. They'd heard about the Galilean who wowed crowds with his insights into God and Scripture, but what did he have to do with them? They were religious, but hardly model synagogue-goers. They knew their way around the Torah, the most important part of the Hebrew Scriptures, but no one was ever going to accuse them of being Pharisees. They kept the Jewish holy days and respected the religious leaders of their village, but they never expected to be asked to teach or hold any office in the synagogue. They were fishermen. They didn't have time to follow the Teacher from Nazareth around as others did. They had work to do—getting their catch to market, keeping their boats and nets in good working order. So, they didn't see it coming—becoming unwitting assistants to Jesus as he stepped into their boat and told them to push off from shore a short way so he could better address the crowd who had gathered to hear him.

They didn't see it coming—the catch, the biggest catch of fish ever taken out of the Sea of Galilee in one casting of nets. When Jesus finished teaching, he told the fishermen to push out into deeper waters and let down their nets. They were skeptical—No, they were *perturbed.* What did this Teacher know about fishing? Besides, they were tired, dog tired, the kind of tired you are when you've worked as hard as you can at something and nothing has produced any results. They'd been fishing all night and come up empty. And what's more, they'd already cleaned and folded their nets. Nevertheless, out of respect for the Teacher, they slowly eased their nets over the sides of the small boat until the edges of them made semi-circles on the surface of the water. Then they gathered in the nets as they'd done hundreds of times before. But, they didn't see it coming—the biggest catch of fish they had ever seen of heard tell of, more than they could get into their boat, so many they had to call for their cousins to bring another boat to hold all the fish.

They most definitely didn't see it coming—the call, the challenge from Jesus that they would become fishers of people. They came from a long line of fishermen. Catching fish is what they knew. It's what they did most days. It's what they were known for. And it's what they expected to do until they were too old and weak to throw out and gather in their nets. They had no other aspirations, thoughts of ever doing anything but catching and selling fish.

The disciples, just before Jesus called them to the grander vision of fishing for men instead of fish, portray most believers today—going about the routines of their faith—going to church and doing church things week after boring week. Even if they have a yearning for more or a hunch that there can be more to being a follower of Jesus, they have no idea what the "something more" could be. But Jesus is there for all of us. He is telling us to push out into deeper waters, challenging us to obey him even when it doesn't make sense, and inviting us to embrace a grander vision.

The true stories that follow show that Jesus is still calling us to follow him, which is not to be confused with becoming immersed in the institutional life of the church. Of all the ways in which we might describe what it means to follow Jesus, surely one on which we can all agree is *lifestyle compassion ministry*.

A Better Paycheck

A saying in the military expresses soldiers' glee at payday. When the paycheck arrives, they say, "The eagle has flown." I know of no similar expression for civilians, but their delight is no less when payday arrives. Most people would say they do not work simply for a paycheck, that they are also motivated by doing something that matters–they may feel their job serves people or produces a product that is useful or adds value to others' lives. Or that their work is one way, maybe the primary way, they find meaning in life. Whatever other motivations or meanings may be attached to one's job, that it produces an income by which we can purchase all the things and services we believe are necessary for our lifestyle is surely one of the most obvious, and that income comes to us in the paycheck.

But what happens when a person's values change? What happens when a person no longer values the things he once valued? What happens when a person finds meaning, fulfillment, purpose, and deep joy in other "things," such as seeing a person gain free access to and from his home for the first time in years because he now has a wheelchair ramp? Or hears a woman who has never had running water tell of her first indoor warm-water bath? Or sees fellow believers discover their ability to make a lasting difference in the lives of strangers, yet neighbors, in their community? What happens then?

One of the things that happens is that "paycheck" is redefined. No longer is it a financial payment for a job done or hours completed "on the job"; it is a feeling of deep, *priceless* happiness. It is a sense that you have touched people at the deepest possible level and that, furthermore, they will never, ever forget what you have done for them. Knowing the positive changes you brought to their lives produces a feeling no money paycheck can ever match.

Mike Moser has experienced this transformation in "payment" for his work—from a conventional paycheck to an emotional and spiritual one. Eight years ago, his church—Mars Hill Baptist Church in Mars Hill, North Carolina, a small college town in the mountains a few miles north of Asheville—did Operation Inasmuch for the first time. He led the one-day event in which about two hundred fellow church members conducted many different compassion ministry projects throughout their community. He says when they finished the day's work, no one asked whether they would do Operation Inasmuch again. That was a given, and everyone knew it. The only questions to be answered had to do with how they would do it better the next time around.

When Moser talks about his life since that first Operation Inasmuch, he does it in terms of a transformation of remuneration: "Seeing a family have a safe, clean home for the first time in a long time, maybe ever, is the best paycheck I could ever receive!" And when you listen to him tell about the many families in the Appalachian hills of Madison County, North Carolina, who have been helped by the Christians both of that community and from elsewhere, you have no doubt that Moser has discovered riches far better than anything he previously knew. Take the example of a little girl named Amber. When she was just an infant, she was terribly burned in an in-home accident. Eventually, she lost both legs and hands, and her face was badly disfigured. Her family lived in a home that was in very poor repair, and they were unable to make the necessary repairs.

In came the good people of Mars Hill Baptist Church. They built a wheelchair ramp so Amber, who depended on a wheelchair for mobility at times, could leave her home. But as often happens when believers give themselves to compassion ministry projects, they discovered that the family had needs that were far more important than whether they had a sound roof over their heads. Amber's father had been nursing deep anger toward God for allowing his little girl to be hurt so badly. It so happened that he was off from work the week the volunteers built the ramp at his home. Through sensitive interaction with him, these faithful followers of Jesus were able to do a little repair work on Amber's father's relationship with God, too. Mike Moser says: "It's great to see this family walk into a church, and now David (the father) tries to work his schedule so he can be off to help when one of the church groups come to help."

Believers have continued their relationship with Amber's family. Says Moser: "I and Mars Hill Baptist Church now have an extended family with the Emersons. Since our first Operation Inasmuch, we and the Community Housing Coalition of Madison County have built a recreational deck, installed a handicap bathroom and remodeled their other bath, remodeled and installed a handicap kitchen, and many other repairs. But we communicate and share beyond the construction times. We have been blessed indeed by being a part of the Emersons' lives."

Mike Moser began a journey of compassion ministry years ago. Operation Inasmuch merely provided the initial foray into compassion ministry, but it ignited something deep inside him that has carried him farther than he imagined. People who knew him well could have predicted this journey. He grew up in a different denomination and followed other generations of his family in becoming a leader of his home church in Asheville. But he was not content merely to "do church" in traditional ways–serving on committees, keeping the institutional machinery working, protecting and preserving the status quo. He became convinced that the church is supposed to be externally focused and dreamed of a time when his church would begin a mission church in their community, one that would have authentic outreach to people who are hurting and disconnected from the God of grace. Unfortunately, he encountered steadfast resistance to his dream and eventually gave up the idea of leading his congregation to face outward and left the church. He left the church but he did not leave that vision of the church being externally focused. His current church family embraced him and his dream and, with Operation Inasmuch, gave him an opportunity to see what that dream might look like in real life.

Today, when he talks about his ministry among the needy families of Madison County, he leans forward, the pace and volume of his voice picks up, and occasionally tears fill his eyes. In other words, his passion is stoked every time he talks about it. A passionate voice describes how he was deeply moved when a project helping a family was completed, partly by profound gratitude that he was part of making a lasting difference in neighbors' lives and partly by his knowledge that many other families in the back roads of Madison County are still waiting for someone to help them. God had launched him on a journey and there was no turning back. He found himself thinking about what could be done to help more families by doing this kind of ministry more often.

After a couple of years of occasional, short-term bursts of compassion ministry, he gathered together representatives of several agencies and nonprofits that deal with housing needs in Madison County. They talked about how they could work together in order to be more effective at what they do. The outcome of these talks was the formation of the Community Housing Coalition of Madison County, which is a unique collection of governmental, faith-based, and nonprofit agencies who specialize in addressing the housing needs of the Appalachian poor. The organization's mission statement serves as much as a *personal* mission statement for Mike Moser as one for the organization:

> To promote decent, safe, affordable housing through advocacy, education, coordination of service and resource development to meet the housing needs of our communities.

Over the years, the Housing Coalition has evolved into an effective organization with an impressive list of accomplishments. The 2006 year-end summary was as follows:

- 924 volunteers
- 39,900 volunteer hours given
- $99,433 given in materials
- $73,000 Home Funds used on 8 homes
- Total of $537,250 invested
- Over 50 families served

The journey continues. As of the writing of this book, he is transitioning into this ministry full-time. He has resigned his work as an insurance agent of ten years to accept the full-time position of Executive Director of the Housing Coalition. His income has taken a downturn, but his paycheck just got bigger! Mike Moser is another person who has been gripped by God's vision of compassion and has taken up a lifestyle of such ministry.

Wheels and Deals

Do you remember your first car? Mine was a royal blue 1968 Volkswagen beetle. My parents helped me buy it when I was in college. Although their financial resources were limited, they helped me purchase a car because I had a job off campus and needed transportation to and from work. That was the rationale, at least. But for me it meant I had fulfilled the first part of the American dream: I was mobile in a culture where mobility is a right of passage.

That car was more than mere transportation for me. It was like a friend. If it's not carrying the personification of material things too far, I could honestly say I loved that car. When I see one like it today (which happens less and less often, and which is why someone gave me a toy model of that car as a gift for Christmas one year) it brings back memories of road trips with friends or visiting my girlfriend out of state or other such romantic recollections. So, the decision to sell the car was possibly the toughest decision of my young life. I found it necessary to pick up a couple of *other* jobs to make the payments on the car and have the money to do the other things I wanted to do as a college student. If I sold the car, I could give up most of my jobs and concentrate on my studies, clearly a major step toward maturity. At that point, I was willing to live with the inconvenience of being without transportation to have a more focused, less cluttered life.

But some form of transportation is hardly a luxury for most people; it's a necessity. There are about 150 million cars in the country compared to about 270 million people.[1] Having an automobile is now a "right of passage" for many youth. At that age it's a luxury, unless, of course, employment is involved, which is why transportation is such a crucial issue for people who do not have it. Then it becomes a *need* on the scale of food, clothing, and shelter.

This is why some churches have begun a car ministry– repairing the automobiles of widows and single parents and, in some cases, giving cars to people who are without transportation. Randy Hodges of Knoxville, Tennessee, began such a ministry in his church.

It all began when Randy became involved in a car clinic project in his church's first Operation Inasmuch. He and others from his Sunday School class performed simple checks on automobiles brought to the church parking lot as part of a larger effort to reach out to the community. Since Randy has enjoyed tinkering with cars for years, this project was "right up his alley." He enjoyed the day immensely not only because it allowed him to do what he most loves to do in his free time but also because it was helping people who needed it.

The next time his church did Operation Inasmuch, he was right there for the car clinic. By the third Operation Inasmuch, Randy was the leader of the Car Clinic Project and still is today. A cadre of people from the church gathered around this project to the point that they often talked about doing this sort of thing at times other than Operation Inasmuch.

Randy and his wife joined sixteen others from the church on a journey to Willow Creek Community Church in Chicago to attend one of their conferences. Randy says he was not at all clear about why he should make that trip, but went out of curiosity. It was there, however, that he learned of a car ministry. Willow Creek has a fully developed car ministry that is nearly full-time and staffed by dozens of volunteers from the church. They repair cars at no cost to the owners and give cars to people who are in dire need of transportation. Although Randy was unable to learn any of the details of Willow's Car Ministry, the concept was firmly planted in his mind.

Conversations with the people whose stories are reported in this book lead me to think that lifestyle compassion ministry, in whatever form it takes, is the germination of a seed idea that has lain dormant for years. The seed was planted by a person of influence or by a personal experience years earlier, and the one-day ministry simply watered and fertilized the ministry seed in the person's heart. A man named Corky was the "person of influence" for Randy. He ran the local service station (back when there was no such thing as self-service). As a teenager, Randy worked at the station, where his love for cars was nourished. More importantly, he saw how Corky helped people as a regular part of his life. When people would stop by asking for "help," he would often give them money out of his own pocket. When the church where he was a member needed someone to respond to a need, they called Corky. He would repair cars that were hardly worth the effort, but because

Corky was sympathetic with people's need for transportation, he would do what he could to help them.

Randy, his father, and brother went with Corky and his son to deliver food baskets to several poor families in their community. Decades later, Randy can still smell the houses where they went. He saw the pieces of coal the families used to heat their homes, which had been picked up from the railroad tracks, where they had fallen off coal trains. They had odds and ends of furniture at best. Randy's eyes were open to the ugly realities of his own community. Through his good friend, Corky, a seed of compassion was planted deep inside Randy that would bear fruit many years later.

A short time after the trip to Willow Creek, Randy came to me, his pastor, to talk about the possibility of having a car ministry through the church. He knew very little about it, but something was stirring in his soul and he was looking for some encouragement. I happily urged him to move forward, to gather interested persons around him, research car ministry, and go forward with the church's blessing.

Fast forward about a year. Randy has gathered a core group of "car ministers." They have defined their mission and researched the ministry by observing another church's ministry. They have positioned themselves to do whatever God leads them to do to provide reliable transportation for people who need it. Along came Bobby, a great-grandmother who has taken on the care of her two great-grandchildren. A church member discovered Bobby through the food pantry ministry of the church. The member was taking food to her because she lacked transportation to come to the pantry. Because the car ministry was made known throughout the church, someone donated a damaged car, which Randy and his team repaired for Bobby.

I was there when Randy gave Bobby the keys to her automobile. You would have thought it was right off the dealer's lot! She was speechless, but managed a simple and heartfelt, "Thank you." Her great-granddaughters were ecstatic. Now they could participate in school events. Bobby could get to the grocery store, the doctor's office, and anywhere else she pleased without concern that her car might break down and leave her stranded again. It was a happy day, but the happiest person was not Bobby; it was Randy Hodges. His ministry seed had germinated, grown up, and born fruit that was a blessing to this elderly woman trying to make the best of what life has dealt her.

As of the writing of this book, the car ministry of Central Baptist Church has given away about ten cars. It is now a respected part of the ministry of the church and rapidly becoming a dependable resource for transportation help in the community. This lifestyle of ministry began with exposure to a contemporary Samaritan named Corky, was stimulated in the Car Clinic of Operation Inasmuch, and will continue to be a blessing to many people in the North Knoxville community.

Friendship as a Ministry

Our cities are full of them. They are one of the many statistics we would rather not hear or much think about. *They* are the thousands of children who grow up in tough circumstances not of their own doing. They are fatherless and sometimes motherless, but they do not live in an institution. They are not wards of the state but exist precariously close to that status. To say they are poor would be an understatement.

Perhaps the saddest truth about these children is that they grow up too fast. In some ways their childhoods do not exist. They are the age of children. Their bodies are small like children's, but their hearts and minds are as tough as whiteleather. Without the love and guidance other children receive in abundance during their developmental years, these children do what they have to in order to survive, and that usually means hardening themselves to their surroundings–their poverty of material things and emotional support, personal dreams, and especially relationships.

When hearing about these children, most people go quickly to the obvious questions: How could life be so unkind as to relegate these little ones to poverty and hopelessness? How can they be helped in ways that do not tax (which is not just a question of money) the rest of too much? What will they be like when they grow up?

Every once in a while, a unique person happens upon a child such as those I have described. None of the above questions come to this person's mind, but rather other questions: What can I do to help this child? What can reach this child and help him or her begin to see realities other than those that bind him or her in hopelessness? Kim Kincer is such a person, and this is her story.

She and a friend gave their time to staff the registration table for one of the opportunities at her church's Operation Inasmuch. Kim and her friend Jo Nance were part of a block party in the neighborhood where dozens of homes were being repaired—from new roofs to painting to numerous other repairs by work crews from as many as twenty churches. The block party was the churches' way of reaching out to the residents of the community while the home repair crews did their thing. The party offered food and fun, especially for children, and it was like a piece of cake attracting ants at a picnic. Children came from everywhere.

Kim and Jo worked at the registration table for a local veterinarian who offered free check-ups for residents' pets. It was an easy job and allowed the two friends to catch up on each other's life. Chyadija was an almost eight-year-old African American girl who spent her day at the block party eating all the food she could hold and taking full advantage of the delightful entertainment of it all. She came over to Kim's table and talked with her several times. She would talk a little, giggle, and run off as if she were embarrassed. She would stay away for a while, but then return for another interchange with these strange white women. Kim tried to get to know Chyadija, but the little girl wouldn't let her in. In Kim's words, "Chyadija had a hard shell around her." In one of her questions of Chyadija, Kim asked what she liked to do and the girl replied: "Beat up my sister."

This was not the sort of thing Kim expected to hear from such a little girl. Kim grew up in Lexington, Kentucky, the daughter of a churchgoing, salt-of-the-earth family. She was shaped by spiritual values that included helping others and doing what you can to make the world a better place. Her parents were positive role models, deeply involved in church and community activities. Her father became passionate about Habitat for Humanity, and Kim worked with him in building Habitat houses in Lexington. Reflecting on her parents' influence, Kim says: "They taught me it's not about me; it's about what the Lord wants us to do."

The neighborhood where Chyadija lived was a different world. To the casual observer, it would appear pride was nonexistent, but that's not true. Chyadija's neighborhood has pride of a different sort. Children are not precious little ones to be cuddled and protected, but people responsible for themselves. Few of the values that shaped Kim's life were present there, at least not as conspicuously as back in her own neighborhood. As a result, Kim's on-and-off conversation with Chyadija that day evoked a growing compassion for this child.

Chyadija's aunt's home was one of the homes being repaired in Operation Inasmuch. Kim made her way to the aunt's home and introduced herself. It was then that she learned that their great-grandmother and great-grandfather were rearing Chyadija and her two siblings—an older sister and younger brother. Their grandmother was "on the street" and, therefore, unable to care for the children. Their mother was also unable to care for the children, who were by three different fathers.

In that brief conversation, something happened that changed Kim's and Chyadija's lives. Kim said to Chyadija: "Let's get together some time. I'll come to see you soon." To which Chyadija replied: "No, you won't." Surprised, Kim asked, "Why would you say that?" And the seven-year-old said: "Because that's what white people do. They say they'll be around but don't."

Something happened to Kim Kincer at that moment. Believers who understand enough of Greek from years of studying the New Testament to know that the ancient language has two words for time, *chronos* and *kairos*—one referring to the ticking of the clock and movement of the calendar and the other referring to defining moments in time—would say Chyadija's response to Kim was a *kairos moment*. That is how Kim describes it. If she doubted her own good intentions to build a friendship with Chyadija before, she didn't after the girl's confrontational response. If she lacked the determination to follow through with her intentions before, she didn't anymore.

The next week Kim called Chyadija's great-grandmother and introduced herself. She asked if she could come see Chyadija. The following week she went to their home. Kim took Chyadija and her older sister, Madisa, who was painfully shy, out to eat. The girls had not been out very much and faced a steep learning curve about appropriate behavior in public places, but Kim was up to the task. From that day forward, Kim was with Chyadija and Madisa at least once a week. She took them shopping, to the park, or to her home for some time away from home for the girls. She took them to Methodist College, where Kim was the women's golf coach. Her relationship with the girls became a cherished ministry for her. Kim's friends, the girls on the golf team at Methodist, and her church friends got involved. The church friends would give Kim money to buy the girls what they needed.

The girls' great-grandparents, who realized she was a source of help that they could not give, accepted Kim. Her relationship with the family grew to the point that Kim actually took the girls to school events. Once Chyadija wanted to be in a school play but did not sign up because it required her to attend practices after school. Without transportation, that was not possible. She asked Kim if she would take her and Kim did.

On three different occasions the school principal called Kim when one of the girls had disciplinary issues. For all practical purposes, this white, Christian woman became Chyadija's and Medisa's surrogate mother. It was a ministry she neither expected nor sought, but when the opportunity presented itself, she embraced it.

Kim Kincer has moved from North Carolina where the events of her story took place and, unfortunately for them, her relationship with Chyadija and Madisa has almost vanished. Their great-grandparents died, and the children were split up among other relatives. Kim lives more than five hundred miles away and has all but lost contact with "her girls." But she is convinced she fulfilled one of God's purposes for her life: to befriend these girls. She did not hear a voice from heaven telling her to take these girls into her life; it was a matter of having the grace of God in her life and wanting to share it with people who need it. Kim did not set out to establish a personal ministry. She was obedient in giving a day of her life in local community ministry at the block party, and God led her into a ministry of friendship. She explains it this way: "Chyadija needed to know someone could love her unconditionally, and I guarantee you that if we could talk to her today, she would tell you that I love her. I think it's important that everyone have that."

Beyond Lifestyle

Most middle-class Anglo Americans maintain safe and familiar traffic patterns. They go and come from school, church, and work along known streets, and seldom venture into the parts of town populated by people in lower socioeconomic circumstances and people who are willing to tolerate, if not encourage, higher crime rates and a drug culture.

Sue Byrd, of Fayetteville, North Carolina, is a noteworthy exception. She often spends the better parts of her days walking up and down streets of neighborhoods in Fayetteville where the people are predominantly African American, of lower socioeconomic status, and often suspicious of white folk. This is her ministry. Sue launched it at the beginning of 2007–Fayetteville Area Operation Inasmuch. The primary purpose of this ministry is to go into the areas of Fayetteville where there is a concentration of needs and arrange for church folk from all over Fayetteville to come on a Saturday and repair many of the homes in that neighborhood. Twice a year since 1995, as many as forty churches throughout Fayetteville, of all denominations and ethnic groups, converge on a neighborhood and conduct dozens of home repair projects. This is accomplished using the popular model of community ministry known as Operation Inasmuch, which began in Fayetteville in 1995 at Snyder Memorial Baptist Church where Byrd is an active member. Until 2007, Byrd led this effort through another local agency. However, she branched out on her own because of restrictions on what the churches could do while repairing the homes, i.e., she was not allowed to give a Bible to the homeowner or pray with people. In establishing her own ministry, she is able to continue the work that she is convinced is her life's purpose. Sue Byrd has moved beyond lifestyle to a calling.

Sue Byrd grew up in Fayetteville and enjoyed the benefits of living in a comfortable, safe, middle-class neighborhood, attending the choice schools of the city, and participating in one of the leading churches. Although her family of origin was middle class, many of her friends shared their opportunities and resources with her. Sue's infectious personality and good looks contributed to her popularity in high school. That she married her high school sweetheart, a jock with success written all over him, only enhanced her future outlook. By the time she graduated from college and began teaching, she was on to bigger and better dreams…except for a couple of developments.

Sue's pastor, Dr. James Cammack, was a warm and affectionate minister whose compassion for people struggling against the forces of oppression led him to preach the grace of God passionately and persistently. Under his preaching, Sue learned not only that she is a person of worth but also that she has the grace of God to pass on to others to help them. That realization was a seed planted deep in her soul that would not germinate for several years, and even more time would pass before it would bear fruit.

A second experience that shaped her future was more of a cultural thing. As a young girl in Fayetteville, she would ride the city buses from her neighborhood to downtown. She noticed African Americans were relegated to the back rows of the bus. While Sue doesn't remember what role the political upheavals around civil rights played in her awareness of the different ways ethnic groups were treated in her youth, it is hard to imagine that they had no effect at all. She remembers wondering to herself why she, a white young girl, was privileged to sit in the front of the bus when the blacks, most of them domestic workers who had put in up to ten hours of working in whites' homes that day, had to sit in the back. The inequality of southern American culture in the '60s made an impression on young Sue that lay dormant, but not dead, for years.

Sue has never been a crusader, but those who know her well attest to her courage and compassion, especially for the disadvantaged. She has playfully been called "compassion in a former cheerleader's body." Both values served her well as she prayerfully considered starting a ministry for which she would have to raise all the funding. She prayed long and hard about that decision. In the beginning she was terrified–not of the people who lived in the neighborhoods where she spent so much of her time, but of the responsibilities of running an independent, parachurch ministry. Ten years of arranging for home repair projects to be done all over Fayetteville gave her confidence that she could do that part of the ministry, although that wasn't enough. There was an office to set up, funds to raise, legal paperwork to complete, funds to raise, a board of directors to recruit, and funds to raise.

The only way she could make the decision to go forward was to know it was God's will for her life. That was the focus of her prayers. Friends encouraged her. They knew her commitment to the poor and marginalized. They believed in her. But she needed to know God was in it.

Byrd received the confirmation she needed in two separate events. The first came on a routine call on a homeowner who called her about having some repairs done on her home. Byrd went to the home to survey the needs. In conversation with the homeowner, she learned that the house had been repaired several years earlier in an Operation Inasmuch. The woman said to her: "Let me show you something." She fetched a Bible that had been given to her when church volunteers repaired her home the last time. The volunteers signed it. She told Sue the Bible didn't mean much to her at the time, but since then she has grown to love its message and the book showed signs of constant use—underlined verses, worn and dog-eared pages. "It was as if God was saying to me: 'This is why you have to do this ministry—because people need to know why believers would give of themselves to help them,'" says Byrd.

The second event came weeks later, when Sue was anxious about how she might find funding to sustain her ministry. She found office space in which to locate her ministry's office for the low rate of $200 per month including utilities, but, as good as the rate was, the funds just weren't there. Two days later she received a check for $2,400–a full year's rent for her office–from a local Presbyterian church. The timing was amazing, but other aspects of the gift were downright awesome. For one thing, the church did not know Sue was contemplating starting the Fayetteville Area Operation Inasmuch. For another, the check was to have been sent six months earlier, but, because of some snafu in the church's bookkeeping, it was delayed until much later in the year–exactly when Sue needed to know that God would provide.

Some people are so stimulated by a one-time, hands-on experience in compassion ministry that they pursue other opportunities to do it. A few are so tuned into God's heartbeat that they make compassion ministry their lifestyle. But rare is the person who transitions from occasional ministry events through a job that has ministerial components all the way to a calling. Sue is a rare Byrd indeed.

The Next Level

Each of these persons has taken ministry to the next level, from "authorized" church activities to personal ministry; from a one-day, low-commitment experience to an ongoing, transformative experience; from occasional, benevolent ministry to lifestyle compassion ministry. Each of them has responded to the urging of God's Spirit to push their boats out into deeper waters to see what God can do with them. They have let down their nets in obedience to Jesus' instructions to use the opportunities God provides to help people in need. Each of them has discovered the grander vision Jesus has for all of his followers.

Mike, Randy, Kim, and Sue are some of my heroes. They inspire me every time I talk with them. They have understood that the compassion ministry to which Jesus calls his followers is not a one-or-two-day-a-year thing. It is a lifestyle. My friends inspire me partly because they have moved into lifestyle compassion ministry *without* the direct leadership or help of their churches. Their pastors (that would be me for Randy and Kim) did not approach them with the challenge to find their own ministries. The deacons did not ask them to take up personal ministries. They did what they have done *on their own*.

This suggests two things: (1) that God is leading individual believers toward lifestyle compassion ministry and (2) that the biblical call to this sort of ministry is *not* something God intends to become a program in the institutional church. Granted, the same thing can be said of any of the New Testament instructions for the church. However, I firmly believe not only that the Spirit of God is capable of moving us into lifestyle compassion ministry without the help of the church, but also that this may well be his strategy. From what I have observed in Mike, Randy, Kim, Sue, and others whose stories I tell in this book, God is leading more and more of his people to be his hands, feet, help, and comfort for people in need. God is drawing believers out of their comfort zones to fulfill Matthew 25 as never before. And God is doing this often without the help of the organized church.

It is time the church becomes a partner in God's ministry to the poor and marginalized. At this point, I must admit that I feel somewhat like the father who has fretted over his rebellious child, then seen the child come around to be more agreeable and make better decisions. Does he seize on the turn of events to hasten the maturing process he sees taking place in the child and risk ruining the child's progress? Or does he keep his distance, trusting that what has begun within the child will continue and *can continue* without his involvement? By urging congregations to take steps to facilitate their members' movement toward lifestyle compassion ministry, will I just muddy the water, or will it become part of what God uses to renew the church?

The fact that you are reading this book shows that I have answered these questions for myself. I have decided to become a partner in the renewal of the church. I am trusting that these pages offer a positive contribution to what God is doing and that God is somehow in the writing and reading of the book.

I realize that not all churches will embrace the message of this book. Some are blind to anything that requires them to divert any of their energy or resources beyond themselves. Others are so conflicted that they cannot comprehend focusing on people in need beyond the walls of their buildings. Most are simply unable to break free from the grip of institutionalism and the accompanying absorption of all energy and resources in traditional programs to do anything new. I am truly sad about these churches and I believe God is, too. In these cases I am convinced God will continue to guide individual believers to find their own personal ministries *despite* the church. Thanks be to God for that. Perhaps God will use the stories of this book to inspire some to follow the examples of Mike Moser, Randy Hodges, Kim Kincer, and Sue Byrd.

If you are one of these people, if something in you is stirred by their stories, if you are willing to push out into the deep waters and let down your nets in pure obedience to Jesus, then read on.

Notes

[1]Partha Dasgupta, "Taming the Automobile," article posted online at http://cactus.eas.asu.edu/partha/Columns/03-26-cars.htm.

2

The Samaritan Way

The first question which the Priest and the Levite asked [on the Jericho Road] was "if I stop to help this man, what will happen to me?" But...the good Samaritan reversed the question: "If I do not stop to help this man, what will happen to him?"

MARTIN LUTHER KING JR.

God created man because he loves stories.

ELIE WIESEL

This book is based on the power of story. Story is the most persuasive form of argument, partly because it doesn't argue at all but merely presents a picture of life, and partly because we naturally identify with almost any story we hear. Here are statements on the power of story from two superb storytellers, Frederick Buechner and Eugene Lowry:

> The power of stories is that they are telling us that life adds up somehow, that life itself is like a story. And this grips us and fascinates us because of the feeling it gives us that if there is meaning in any life–in Hamlet's, in Mary's, in Christ's–then there is meaning also in our lives.[1]

> Anytime you tell a story, you open the door for metaphor to operate. When, for example, you describe the apprehension a child experiences in moving to a new school,

you have done more than describe moving to a new school. You have produced a metaphor that touches images of apprehension throughout the congregation. You may not have intended to address that person who is about to retire from the railroad...and that person may not be able to identify just what the connection was, but impact–however undefined propositionally–happened.[2]

Stories have a way of bringing us together. They create community. People who tell each other stories become friends, and the more they share with each other, the deeper their relationships grow. Story evokes emotional responses–joy, sadness, anxiety, fear, love, and so forth. It is a powerful stimulus for emotions. As a result, story has the power to teach, console, and persuade better than other forms of communication. Bruce Salmon puts it this way: "We may learn more vicariously from a story in the span of a few minutes than we learn experientially from life in the span of months or years. What begins as pleasure ends in truth."[3]

One of the best examples of the power of story in the Bible is the case of Nathan's confronting David with his sin (2 Sam. 12). After David allowed his lust for Bathsheba to drive him to arrange for her husband's death so he could have her for himself, Nathan went to David to let him know of God's anger for what he had done. But instead of confronting King David straight out, he told him a story about a rich man who stole the single lamb of a poor man for a meal by which to entertain a house guest. David failed to see the connection of the story with his own sin and raged angrily against the greed and crime of the rich man in Nathan's story. At that moment the prophet said, "You are that man!" and there was nothing David could do to avoid the painful exposure of his sin. However, as a result of this confrontation, David's relationship with God was repaired and some of the most moving parts of Scripture were written (see Ps. 32).

In examining the role of story historically in church life, Thomas Boomershine reminds us that the gospel was originally a storytelling tradition. Only later was it conveyed primarily through writing. Even the word *gospel* can be traced in English to the phrase "good tale." Boomershine says: "In Old English, therefore, the word that was the best equivalent for the Latin word *evangelium* was a tale whose telling had power."[4] So, from the literal meaning of the word *gospel* to persons' experiences with stories, story has played a prominent role in church life, empowering people to encounter truth.

Jesus was a master storyteller, actually *the* Master Storyteller. His stories are some of the best-known parts of his public ministry. Although they are old, their plots are anachronistic, and they may not measure up to twenty-first–century standards of what makes for a good story (i.e., no Internet linkage or interactive video), these stories still work. They still persuade, convict, and motivate. And none of Jesus' stories is more persuasive, convicting, or motivating than the parable of the Good Samaritan. Any book that has as its purpose to lead believers and congregations into a lifestyle of compassion ministry *must* give this story center stage. By titling this book *The Samaritan Way,* I have tried to do more than that; I am suggesting that this story become the foundation of Christian compassion ministry.

I am convinced that Jesus told this story to do just that. At first, it appears that Jesus told it simply to answer a man's question about what it means to love one's neighbor. It was merely a clever and cogent reply to what had probably become a thorny theological issue–namely, what does it mean to love your neighbor as you love yourself? But Jesus was looking far beyond that question when he told this story. His perspective was always greater than the immediate situation. He was thinking about the millions of victims of injustice, war, and poverty who would populate this planet as long as it exists, and what God wants his people to do for them. He was thinking about the disabled, the neglected, the oppressed, and the sick who are hurting and hopeless. He was thinking about the responsibility they represent for the strong, the affluent, and the powerful. When Jesus told the parable of the Good Samaritan, he was establishing a timeless, perfect model of compassion ministry.

We know this not only because it fits how Jesus generally did ministry–using the immediate situation to teach for the long-term–but also because this powerful story has inspired compassion ministry for nearly twenty centuries. Think of all the hospitals named after it. Think of the many ministries that have tapped into its truth by using *Samaritan* in their name, the largest such of our time being Samaritan's Purse, Franklin Graham's ministry of compassion for children in Third World countries. I do not think it is an exaggeration to say that this one story has inspired and informed more compassion ministry than any other piece of human communication.

The Story Still Speaks

In the early '90s, Robert Wuthnow of Princeton University conducted a comprehensive study of what Americans think about compassion and how they are involved in acts of compassion. He published his findings in *Acts of Compassion*. He devotes a significant portion of his book to the influence of the parable of the Good Samaritan on Americans' thought and acts of compassion. Here is what he says about the influence of this simple story:

> It is a simple story, and so, even with all our sophistication in science and technology, we hark back to it. We can remember it and retell it. We see examples in our daily lives that bring it to our minds. It is taught by religious institutions, along with all the subtle doctrines and theologies we cannot remember. It is also reinforced in the secular media through television stories and literary narratives that build on its simple outline. Jim Casey in *The Grapes of Wrath* is the Good Samaritan. So is the Lone Ranger. Mother Teresa is the dusty streets of Calcutta and Albert Schweitzer on the muddy trails of Africa are too. The Good Samaritan is the legendary figure who helps someone else along the road. The story is one of those ancient myths that embodies the deepest meanings in our culture. In learning it and reshaping it we define what it means to be compassionate.[5]

That last line—"it...define[s] what it means to be compassionate"— summarizes the influence of this wonderful story. In marketing parlance, the Good Samaritan has become a recognizable brand in our culture. The mere word *Samaritan* conveys the meaning of compassionate caring for others. So, it is not surprising that Wuthnow found a positive relationship between those who know something about the story and compassionate behavior. In his survey he found that "two-thirds of those who were currently involved in charity or social-service activity knew the story, compared to only four in ten among those who were not currently involved."[6]

The story of the Good Samaritan has been retold in more ways than can be counted. Many preachers have contemporized the story to help their congregations get past their familiarity with it so it speaks to them where they are. Wuthnow found any number of people who could tell parts of the story without knowing much about where it came from or the context of its origination. One such person was Ted Garvey, a former Peace Corps volunteer who works with the mentally ill homeless. He knew the story even though he had not been to church since his childhood. He retold it in a way that relates to his work with homeless persons:

> A man is lying on the sidewalk in the grip of some psychosis or drug-induced catatonia, and he's asking people for help, and people pass by him, and then someone comes by who recognizes the man as suffering from what he's suffering from. They see certain psychotic symptoms. And through compassion or whatever, and through a certain amount of knowledge and information about community resources or whatever, can try to help the man out, walk him down the street to a project or call a detox center. Those would be little steps, but do anything rather than just walking by.[7]

Whereas the parable of the Good Samaritan is so well known that it is no longer the exclusive "property" of the Christian church (if, indeed it ever was), church is still the place where most people hear it and learn from it. Wuthnow found that among those who attend church weekly, 88 percent had heard a sermon on loving their neighbors within the past year compared to only 40 percent of those who attended less than once a month. "Moreover, by a margin of 61 percent to 30 percent, those who said they had heard a sermon on loving their neighbors were more likely than those who had not heard a sermon to say they could tell the story of the Good Samaritan."[8] Wuthnow found that going to church and hearing the parable of the Good Samaritan had a definite effect of helping persons be compassionate toward people in need.

This is one of the easiest arguments I will make in this book—that the parable of the Good Samaritan is a model of lifestyle compassion ministry for all time. Therefore, it would be tempting simply to make that point and move on without allowing the story to do its work yet again. But to do so would be to miss the opportunity to let Jesus move us closer to his goal for us—namely, to be fully devoted followers living life as he lived it. So, the remainder of this chapter will be given to a thorough examination of this story of stories, exposing ourselves to its penetrating power.

The Story

And a lawyer stood up and put Him to the test, saying, "Teacher, what shall I do to inherit eternal life?" And He said to him, "What is written in the Law? How does it read to you?" And he answered, "YOU SHALL LOVE THE LORD YOUR GOD WITH ALL YOUR HEART, AND WITH ALL YOUR SOUL, AND WITH ALL YOUR STRENGTH, AND WITH ALL YOUR MIND; AND YOUR NEIGHBOR AS YOURSELF."

And He said to him, "You have answered correctly; DO THIS AND YOU WILL LIVE."

But wishing to justify himself, he said to Jesus, "And who is my neighbor?"

Jesus replied and said, "A man was going down from Jerusalem to Jericho, and fell among robbers, and they stripped him and beat him, and went away leaving him half dead. And by chance a priest was going down on that road, and when he saw him, he passed by on the other side. Likewise a Levite also, when he came to the place and saw him, passed by on the other side.

"But a Samaritan, who was on a journey, came upon him; and when he saw him, he felt compassion, and came to him, and bandaged up his wounds, pouring oil and wine on them; and he put him on his own beast, and brought him to an inn, and took care of him. And on the next day he took out two denarii and gave them to the innkeeper and said, 'Take care of him; and whatever more you spend, when I return I will repay you.' Which of these three do you think proved to be a neighbor to the man who fell into the robbers' hands?"

And he said, "The one who showed mercy toward him." Then Jesus said to him, "Go and do the same." (Lk. 10:25–37 NASB)

Negative Models

The story of the Good Samaritan teaches and inspires compassion, but in a more general sense, it teaches priorities according to Jesus. The Samaritan is not the only model in the story. The Priest and Levite provide negative models. In more recent times, persons who failed to respond to a victim with compassion have attracted even more attention, such as in the well-publicized and studied case of Kitty Genovese. In 1964 a young woman named Kitty Genovese was stabbed to death on the streets of New York City. That hardly made the headlines of the morning paper. However, that Genovese was chased and attacked three times on the streets over the course of half an hour *as thirty-eight of her neighbors watched from their windows without any of them calling the police or trying to intervene on her behalf* did make the news. The case became symbolic of cold, dehumanizing city life. As Abe Rosenthal, who would later become editor of *The New York Times*, wrote a book about the case, said:

> Nobody can say why the thirty-eight did not lift the phone while Miss Genovese was being attacked, since they cannot say themselves. It can be assumed, however, that their apathy was indeed one of the big-city variety. It is almost a matter of psychological survival, if one is surrounded and pressed by millions of people, to prevent them from constantly impinging on you, and the only way to do this is to ignore them as often as possible. Indifference to one's neighbor and his troubles is a conditioned reflex in life in New York as it is in other big cities.[9]

The Genovese case and the mountain of commentary it provoked have kept alive an ongoing debate about whether people should get involved in helping others in need, especially in distress. Studies were conducted on what became known as the "bystander problem." Bibb Lane of Columbia University and John Darley of New York University conducted a series of studies to try to understand this problem. They staged emergencies of one kind or another in various situations to see who would come and help. Surprisingly, they found that when a person encounters an emergency alone, that is, that no one else is around at all, he or she is more likely to respond. But when several people encounter the same emergency, they are less likely to respond. In one experiment, people who saw smoke seeping out from under a doorway would report it 75 percent of the time when they were on their own, but only 38 percent of the time when they were in a group. Lane and Darley concluded that when people are in a group, responsibility for acting is diffused. They assume someone else will make the call, or they assume that when no one else is responding, the apparent problem isn't really a problem.[10]

Another study, this one by Darley and a colleague at Princeton Theological Seminary, found that a person's context influences whether or not that person will stop to help a person in distress. They created a situation in which seminarians would encounter a man bent over, coughing and giving the impression he was in trouble and watched to see which young theologians stopped. They added the variable of telling some of the students to prepare a short talk on the parable of the Good Samaritan and others on a totally different subject. Then they told some they were running late so they should hurry to give their talk and others that they had plenty of time. Of those running late, whether they had just reread the parable of the Good Samaritan or not, only 10 percent stopped to help the man. Of those who had time, *63 percent stopped.* Having sufficient time mattered more than preparing for ministry or preparing to talk to others about the Good Samaritan.[11]

I do not doubt the validity of these studies, but, as interesting as they may be, they miss the point. From the standpoint of the victim, our reasons for not responding do not matter. Suffering still victimizes people. Crime still hurts people. Kitty Genovese is still dead. Her family and friends will grieve her death for a long time. And the city of New York has a permanent black eye.

Besides, I cannot imagine that Jesus would react to these studies by saying, "You've found it! You've finally discovered the secret to why the Priest and Levite did not stop to help the victim by the side of the Jericho Road."

Priorities

I am intrigued by these two men who passed up their chance to be a hero and hurried on their way. Did they wonder whether they did the right thing in passing by without so much as lifting a finger to help, or were they so programmed not to defile themselves that they hardly gave it a thought? Did their guts tighten the next time they prayed for the downtrodden? Did they tell their wives what happened when they got home that night, or were they too ashamed to mention it? Did they lie awake at night unable to close their eyes, because every time they did images of a beaten, bloody man tormented them? Were they reminded of their failure every time thereafter they traveled the Jerusalem-Jericho Turnpike? Did they use this situation as a case study in teaching Jewish young men the importance of discipline—not to give in to questionable needs where there is a chance of ceremonial defilement? How did these two deal with their part in the story?

I am sure they did not set out to be cold and indifferent. In their minds, they had good reasons for not stopping to help the victim. That is precisely what Jesus wants us to see in them—people who *choose not* to be compassionate because they have wrong priorities—and he was intentional in having the passersby be a Priest and a Levite, one a religious leader by profession and the other a lay religious leader. Obviously, Jesus constructed this story to speak first to the Jewish leader who engaged him in the first place, but in a larger sense he wanted to confront future religious folk, either professionals or otherwise, who make the mistake of confusing church work with the work of the church.

This shift in priorities comes so subtlety and gradually that we do not realize it has happened until it is done. Before we know it, our whole life direction has changed. Those things we said in our early days of vision and dreams were essential, nonnegotiable, and all-consuming have been forgotten, or at least set aside for another time, which rarely comes.

How can this happen? How can we let ourselves be swallowed up by compromise? For most of us, the culprit is our desire to succeed. As long as we were committed to high ideals, success didn't matter. Doing the right thing was the engine that drove us. Then, gradually we moved over into the ranks of those striving to succeed by the culture's standards of what it means to be successful. Compassion ministry does not rank very high on that list. Stephen Vincent Benet said it right:

Life is not lost by dying.
Life is lost
Minute by minute
day by dragging day,
In all the thousand
small uncaring ways.

This shift in priorities can also happen to churches. The phenomenon has been studied for some time now. First, there is a need or network of needs, and then a charismatic leader or a group of leaders arise to meet them. These leaders have a clear vision of the needs and articulate them better than anyone else, so people begin to follow them and the movement is born. At this stage everything is open and fluid. Nothing is restricted. Everyone is inventive and hard working. The organization is loose and adaptive. There is also very little money. There are no institutional salaries, no full-time secretaries, and there is little property to worry about. The important thing is spirit. Spirit rules over everything. It is the surest guarantee of success.

If the movement succeeds, it begins to exhibit different characteristics. It passes through several stages on the way to being institutionalized. First, it loses sight of the needs for which it came into being because it has developed its own needs. Second, it grows beyond the need for a charismatic leader and acquires a CEO (Chief Executive Officer), someone with more poise, more diplomacy, and more stability than the original leader. At the same time, the institution becomes enormously complicated and must tighten its organizational structures. It acquires property, develops staff, and draws up flow charts to show who is responsible to whom. Now the operative word is no longer *spirit* but *budget.*

Can you see how all this applies to the church? The early church began as a movement. At some point, the exact time of which church historians are still debating, it became an institution. Individual churches almost always begin as movements and inevitably they become institutions. Ministers commit themselves to what they perceive as the movement of the Christian life, which includes lifestyle compassion ministry. However, at some point they realize they have really joined an institution, something with traditions, rules, budgets, and expectations. Even if they have imagined themselves as charismatic leaders, they learn churches much prefer CEOs, leaders who operate by consensus and permission rather than from instinct, compassion, or love.

This is when we act like the Priest and Levite in the story of the Good Samaritan. We've been programmed not to think or act on our own. We are representatives of a public institution. So we conduct ourselves in ways we think will best represent the institution.

This is how priorities get screwed up. And it can happen so easily. In a church where I once served as pastor, there was a weekend discipleship emphasis for teenagers. About forty teens went through a special course of study that had the potential of solidifying their relationship to Jesus, if not propelling them forward in a new spurt of spiritual growth. From what I could see, it was a splendid experience for all involved–youth and adults alike. The youth minister and I talked about it a few days later, when he shared with me his disappointment that some in the church had missed the point of the weekend experience. Rather than comment on this major event for the teens, a parent of one of the youth raked the youth minister over the coals that very Sunday for not writing in the church newsletter that the boys' basketball team had won the championship of their league.

What does all this have to do with the story of the Good Samaritan? Just this: when we lose our vision of what it means to be followers of Jesus because institutional demands have sucked the life out of us (either as individual believers or as congregations), we are like the Priest and Levite who had better things to do than get their hands dirty in helping the poor victim by the side of the Jerusalem-Jericho Road. Whatever they were about, it did not come from the kind of love for God called for in the Hebrew Shema (which the Jewish leader quoted to Jesus in verse Lk. 10:27). And it certainly bore no resemblance to neighborly love. Compassion is God's heartbeat and it is to be our priority.

Lessons from a Compassionate Stranger

Okay, the examples of bad behavior have had enough print. Jesus gives a compelling example of compassion ministry in the person of the Samaritan who stopped and helped the robbery victim. Let's take a long, hard look at this man and see what Jesus intends for us to learn from him.

The most conspicuous thing about him is his ethnic identity. As a Samaritan, he was the least likely person a Jew would have expected in Jesus' time to do what he did. It would be like seeing a member of Al Qaida stop to help a suffering Orthodox Jew in our time. Of course, Jesus said this deliberately. The Samaritan's ethnicity and the history of Jewish-Samaritan relations meant he had no obligation to stop and give aid. No law, no social convention, and no religious prescription dictated that he render help. Yet he stopped. Why? That is precisely the question Jesus is pulling out of us. He has constructed the story so as to provoke that very question.

The lesson for us here is that compassion ministry will inevitably do the same thing. It will provoke the question, "Why?" In compassion ministry, we are about more than meeting immediate needs. We are concerned with the whole person—his or her spiritual and emotional well-being, as well as the physical needs. But we are often held at arm's length in relating to persons' nonphysical needs. People are reluctant to let us into that part of their lives. However, when we show them we care for them by ministering to their physical needs, they trust us and let us into the more private realms of their lives. They often open that door when they ask us why we would help them.

When I share the Operation Inasmuch model of community ministry with a congregation, I tell the story of one project in which church volunteers gave $1 bills to people pumping gas at a self-service gas station. Although $1 doesn't make much of a dent in a person's fuel bill, it is highly irregular for a total stranger to give away money. So, most of those given the $1 bills asked "Why?" And each time the volunteers said, "This is Operation Inasmuch, a day when our church members are out in the community showing people that God loves them and we do, too." One man who heard that answer immediately shared about his grandchild in a special care unit at Vanderbilt Hospital in Nashville, Tennessee. The volunteer who gave him the money gathered his friends around the man and they prayed for his grandchild and for him.

The biblical support for this model is 1 Peter 3:13, 15: "Who is going to harm you if you are eager to do good?...Always be prepared to give an answer to everyone who asks you to give the reason for the hope that you have."

Jesus answers the why question when he says that the Samaritan man had compassion on the victim. I intentionally chose to use a translation of the parable that uses the word *compassion.* Other translations use other words. *Compassion* is the best word to describe ministry to persons in need, and Jesus provides a picture of compassion in the story of the Good Samaritan.

Compassion is an intrinsic value, not an acquired skill or attitude. Jesus makes compassion the story's pivot. The story turns on the Samaritan's compassion. He stopped when the others did not because he had compassion. Whatever his destination or the reason for his journey to Jericho, it took a back seat to the circumstances he encountered in the victim's condition. Because of his compassion, the Samaritan asked not, "What will happen to *me* if I stop?" which is what the Priest and Levite probably asked themselves, but, "What will happen to *this man* if I do not stop?" Because of his compassion, the victim lived. And because of his compassion, untold numbers of people since have been inspired to help strangers "on the way."

Where does compassion come from? Is it a value only some people have, or may anyone have it? I believe the most accurate answer is that compassion comes from God. He has endowed us with the capacity to be moved by another's pain. Compassion is part of the character of God. Scripture makes it abundantly clear that God is merciful and compassionate. He is moved by humanity's pain and suffering, even by their rebellion and disobedience. So, one explanation of the basic capacity for compassion is that it is part of what it means to have been created in God's image. Compassion is one quality of the human existence that separates us from the rest of the created order. What I am saying is that all persons have the capacity for compassion. However, some have developed that capacity more fully. The Priest and Levite in Jesus' story either suppressed their feelings of compassion because of what they perceived to be more pressing issues or because of traditional views of cleanliness. But the Samaritan's compassion was strong enough to stop him and to override any concerns he may have had about getting involved, even though his standing as a Samaritan meant he could not be expected to help a Jew.

Compassion can be cultivated just like love can be cultivated. Whereas the basic capacity is a gift from God, the power and influence of that gift is determined by how we exercise it. Think of it as a spiritual muscle. Unused and undeveloped, it can atrophy. It can become as useless as an arm that is bound to the torso for a long time. But when it is exercised, when it is used often and rigorously, it grows stronger. Any believer has the necessary compassion to develop a lifestyle of ministry to persons in need, and, furthermore, such a lifestyle will not diminish life at all, but will rather enrich and enhance it.

Compassion responds naturally to whatever need it encounters. The pain of others triggers compassion. It responds naturally, just as the body does with an instant infusion of adrenaline into the bloodstream when danger is sensed. Compassion does not need to be "worked up," but needs merely the stimulus of another's pain to move a person into action. Such is the picture of the Samaritan is Jesus' story.

The key is *seeing*–seeing the other person's pain, having an awareness of the realities of another's suffering. Clearly, the Samaritan saw what the Priest and Levite did not see. They too saw the injured man. Jesus says they passed by him so as to avoid him as much as possible–"on the other side of the road." But they did not see what might become of the man if they did not stop to help him. The Samaritan did. That was all he saw–the man's pain and need.

Seeing is often the difference in one person acting out of compassion and another not acting in the same situation. This is reminiscent of another incident in Jesus' public ministry. A woman of ill repute came to him when he was in the home of a Pharisee. Although at the time it was a gross violation of social protocol for any woman to approach a man in this way, she anointed Jesus' feet. For allowing her to do this, the Jewish leaders criticized Jesus roundly. His response was to ask: "Do you see this woman?"

Scientists have studied the phenomenon of not seeing what is in front of you. The Visual Cognition Lab at the University of Illinois conducted an experiment in which subjects watched a one-minute video of two teams of three players each. One team wore black shirts and the other team wore white shirts, and the players moved around one another in a tight circle, tossing two basketballs. The subjects were asked to count the number of passes made by the white team–not an easy task given the interweaving movement of the players. After thirty-five seconds and out of the blue, someone dressed in a gorilla costume entered the circle, walked directly into the midst of the weaving players, thumped his chest, and nine seconds later exited out of the circle and out of view.[12]

Here is the amazing part. Fifty percent of the subjects did not see the gorilla. They were so caught up in counting the passes of the basketball they never saw the gorilla. The victim in the parable of the Good Samaritan might as well have been that gorilla. The Priest and Levite did not really see him.

Compassion overcomes barriers to minister to another's need. The difference between pity and compassion is action. Pity is an emotional response to the sight of human pain–like the fleeting feeling that comes over us just before we reach for the remote when a commercial presents a vivid picture of starving children, or the emotional cringe we feel when walking past a homeless man sleeping on the sidewalk or a park bench. Pity is barely related to compassion. It is the feeling James had in mind when he wrote: "Suppose a brother or sister is without clothes and daily food. If one of you says to him, 'Go, I wish you well; keep warm and well fed,' but does nothing about his physical needs, what good is it?" (Jas. 2:15–16). Perhaps the Priest and Levite felt pity for the victim by the side of the road, but they did not feel compassion or they would have stopped to help the man in need.

Compassion is about action. The temptation here is to distinguish one kind of compassion from another–true compassion versus false; authentic versus phony–but I will resist that temptation by saying that compassion is compassion. The Samaritan had it and the others did not. He had it not only because Jesus says he had it, but because he stopped. He acted, and *that* is the evidence. The Samaritan overcame several barriers to help the victim.

He overcame the barrier of fear. What if the robbers who did this to the man had left him there as "bait" for other unsuspecting or naïve travelers? What if the man died while the Samaritan was helping him? What if someone else came along and assumed that he, the Samaritan, was responsible for the crime? We will never know whether the Samaritan was aware of any of these fears but it is hard to imagine that he was oblivious to them. Nevertheless, he stopped. None of these fears was enough to supersede his compassion for the dying man.

He overcame the barrier of ethnicity. So much has been made of the hatred between the Samaritans and the Jews that I hardly need to expound on what was a gigantic rift between these neighbors on the scale of Sunni-Shiite relations in modern-day Iraq. Suffice it to say that it was news any time a Jew and a Samaritan were *civil* to each other, much less one helping the other when he had a choice. Of the three who passed by the victim in Jesus' story, the Samaritan had far more reasons not to stop than anyone else. But he stopped...because he had compassion. And Jesus wants us to see what compassion does: it overcomes barriers to act.

I want to drill down on this point a bit because it is crucial to the purpose for this book. Compassion *acts.* It may begin with an emotion, but it inevitably leads to some sort of action. *Lifestyle compassion ministry is active involvement in others' pain, either directly or indirectly.* Consider these examples.

A young girl was bullied and ridiculed because she suffers from epilepsy. Her parents moved her to another school, hoping she could escape the cruelty of the students in her former school, but it didn't work. The bullying began again. Some students even launched a Web site where fellow bullies could spew their hatred against this girl, just because she is different. The girl thought about taking her own life many times. Then, two girls in her school decided to do something about this mistreatment. They started a campaign of writing encouraging notes to the victimized girl. They got their friends to join them and their friends got their friends involved. Soon there was a movement that totally changed the epileptic girl's life. Compassion acts.

Two older children were moved by the sacrifices American servicemen and women are making in the Iraq war. As they heard stories of military families suffering from long absences of their father/husband, they decided to act. They began a campaign to provide phone cards to servicemen and women in Iraq and Afghanistan. Soon the campaign spread far beyond their neighborhood and even beyond their own town. It is now a national movement of compassion. Compassion acts.

On April 4, 1975, days before the fall of Saigon, a U.S. jet carrying 243 Vietnamese orphans crashed into the Asian jungle. A third of the children burned to death while many of the remaining victims were critically injured. The Pentagon said it would not have the resources to rescue the children for at least ten days.

Robert Macauley, a paper broker in New Canaan, Connecticut, saw the story on television. No stranger to pain and difficulty in his own life, he was deeply moved by the plight of these children. With more pluck than common sense, he pulled together the little money he could and arranged to charter a Boeing 747 to rescue the young survivors. Within forty-eight hours the children were delivered safely to their adoptive parents. The rescue plan was a success—but then Macauley had to deal with financial realities. He didn't have the $10,000 in the bank to cover the down payment for the aircraft. (The check he wrote bounced.) Nor did he have the $241,000 for the balance still owed. To cover the cost, the Macauleys took out a mortgage on their house. "It was a fair trade," Mrs. Macauley said. "The bank got the house and Bob got the kids."

Bob Macauley's unbounded compassion and sheer audacity led to the founding of the organization AmeriCares. Over the past twenty-five years. AmeriCares has delivered more than $3.4 billion in aid to 137 countries. The hallmark of its success is Bob Macauley's impatience with bureaucracy. "You act now, and worry about red tape later." Macauley is a Samaritan-like character. I don't know if he knows Jesus, but I do know that Jesus knows him. He is a fine, contemporary example of compassion that acts.[13]

Compassion sees it through. Compassion does not look for the easy way. It is intent on the right way. The Samaritan did not bind up the man's wounds and walk away telling himself he'd done his part and someone else would have to take it from there. It might have been quite a while before another compassionate soul passed that way. The man needed shelter and additional care. So, he loaded him into his "Chevy" and took him to the nearest hotel. The Samaritan stayed with the man through the night, probably rechecking the man's wounds, giving him water and wine and otherwise tending to his needs. Before he went on his way the next day, he gave the innkeeper money to ensure that the beaten man would receive all the care he needed. The Samaritan's compassion was thorough.

In responding to another's pain, the objective is to alleviate that pain, not to put a bandage on it, brush one's hands together, and say, "That's that!" Compassion is a ministry of engagement. It looks for ways to end pain, not merely medicate it for a while. This book is a call to lifestyle compassion ministry, not to a hit-and-run approach or occasional bursts of mercy. It calls us all to pitch our tent where it hurts and stay until the job is done.

To this point, I have attempted to draw out of the story of the Good Samaritan what compassion *does*. It is an intrinsic value; it responds naturally to any need it encounters; it overcomes barriers; it acts; it sees help through. There is one final lesson about compassion to be gleaned from this story: *Compassion is messy.*

Compassion is the response of followers of Jesus to people's pain, and pain is hardly neat and clean. It's bloody and dirty and smelly and ugly. It was for the Samaritan and it is for us. I doubt very much that there was a white square with a red cross painted on the side of his donkey. That is to say, he did not go looking for someone to help that day. But when he encountered a man lying by the side of the road, bloody and dirty from having been beaten nearly to death by robbers, he stopped. It was a messy situation, but not too messy for his compassion.

The physical challenges of the circumstances in Jesus' story are representative of the messiness of compassion ministry. There are real dangers. And in our world there are even more dangers. We have all heard stories of persons who have helped a victim "by the road" only to be sued later. To help, people have to be willing to get their hands dirty, their hearts pricked, and their futures jeopardized.

Recently, I attended a conference designed to inspire individual Christians and congregations to get more involved in compassion ministry. Most of the plenary session speakers reminded the audience that compassion ministry is messy. It was not a warning, but an acknowledgment of reality. Helping people with one need often leads to other needs. I remember a phone call I received from a man in my community. I was a pastor at the time, but the caller was not a member of my church nor had we ever met. He was an insurance agent in the community and he'd encountered a family with lots of needs. He called me because our church had become known in the community as one that helps people. He said his church could not help this family but he was hoping we could.

I took down the name and phone number of the head of the household in the family—the grandmother who was the only employed person in the three-member family. Her daughter was suffering from mental illness and emotional issues. Her grandson was mentally challenged and unable to function normally. The grandmother was trying her best to hold this poor family together.

I asked some women in the church to look into the situation. They suggested that we help them move. The grandmother had just purchased a home and needed help moving their things from an apartment to the house. Several of us gave the better portion of a Saturday to move this family and help them clean up the old apartment. We were done in one day. Right? Wrong! Compassion is messy.

In the course of moving them, we discovered several other needs. They needed several pieces of furniture, so church members donated furniture they could use. Their van needed repairing, so the church's car ministry spent several days repairing the vehicle. Neighbors next to their new house tormented their dog, so members built a fence for them to provide added security for the family. And throughout all of this, more than a little money was given to help the family get a new start. What was to be a one-time project became an ongoing ministry because compassion is messy—*but it's the right thing to do!*

Go and Do Likewise

At the beginning of this chapter I said Jesus' intention in giving the parable of the Good Samaritan was to provide an enduring model of compassion ministry and to inspire all generations of God's people to follow the Samaritan's example of lifestyle compassion ministry. The answer to the question Jesus posed at the end of the parable—"Which of these was neighbor to the man?"—was obvious, but it gave him the opportunity to tell the man: "Go and do likewise."

And so it is for us. Jesus expects us to do likewise, too. We can't hear this story (or any story of compassion ministry, for that matter) without feeling the need to do what the Samaritan did. Story has that kind of power.

In his study of compassion in American culture, Robert Wuthnow comes to an interesting conclusion:

> I am aware that many people value compassion because they have been taught to in their churches, synagogues, fellowship halls, and meeting places. I am also aware that these organizations command valuable resources for mobilizing people, turning their good intentions into concrete actions, so that the needy are actually helped... [Religious people] are able to recount the stories they have heard, such as the story of the Good Samaritan. And these stories probably have a power we need to rediscover and understand more fully. But the way most people understand the Good Samaritan leaves them with little more than the admonition "go and do likewise.[14]

What else needs to be said?

Notes

[1]Frederick Buechner, *The Magnificent Defeat* (New York: Seabury Press, 1966), 60, as cited by Bruce Salmon, *Storytelling in Preaching* (Nashville: Broadman, 1988), 38.

[2]Eugene Lowry, *Doing Time in the Pulpit* (Nashville: Abingdon Press, 1985), 91, as cited by Salmon, *Storytelling in Preaching*, 38.

[3]Salmon, *Storytelling in Preaching*, 39.

[4]Thomas E. Boomershine, *Story Journey* (Nashville: Abingdon Press, 1988), 16.

[5]Robert Wuthnow, *Acts of Compassion: Caring for Others and Helping Ourselves* (Princeton: Princeton University Press, 1991), 160–61.

[6]Ibid., 161.

[7]Ted Garvey, as quoted in ibid., 166–67.

[8]Ibid., 177.

[9]Cited by Malcolm Gladwell, *Tipping Point: How Little Things Can Make a Difference* (New York: Little, Brown and Co., 2000), 27.

[10]Ibid., 28.

[11]Ibid., 163–65.

[12]For further information, see an article by Daniel J. Simons, one of the scientists involved in the Univ. of Illinois experiment, at http://www.scholarpedia.org/article/Inattentional_blindness.

[13]For more information on Bob Macauley, see *His Name is Today: Bob Macauley and Americares* (Ottawa, Ill.: Jameson Books, 2005).

[14]Wuthnow, *Acts of Compassion*, 284–85.

3

It's Not about Us

Nothing gives a more spuriously good conscience than keeping rules, even if there has been a total absence of real charity and faith.

C. S. LEWIS

I have heard it said that if young ministers can survive their first church after seminary, they *might* have what it takes to be a finisher. Typically, preachers fresh out of seminary are long on dreams and plans and short on practical experience. Typically, their first place of ministry is one that is about as suitable for such dreams as a fur coat is for a Caribbean vacation in July. Churches that hire freshly ordained ministers as their pastor tend to be small, old but unaware of it, more or less happy with the status quo, and ignorant of the latest trends in ministry and proud of it. In other words, they make success in terms familiar to the new pastor so impossible that he or she can hardly escape the situation without questioning his or her call to ministry. And some do not come up with favorable answers to such questions.

I know, because that was my experience—well, almost. When I graduated from seminary in the spring of 1978, I went to a large, downtown church in the deep South. My responsibilities were divided between this large, affluent, rock-of-the-community congregation and a small, dying, inwardly focused congregation.

A few years earlier the small congregation petitioned the large church to "take them over." The small church would deed their property and give all their offerings to the large church in exchange for pastoral leadership. This leadership would be in the person of an associate pastor who had duties at the large church while also serving as pastor of the smaller church. I know it sounds strange, but this was the context of my first ministry position out of seminary.

Predictably, I threw myself into the pastoral role for the small congregation of about fifty-to-sixty people with all of the enthusiasm of a child on Christmas morning. I believed my passion would jump-start that sleepy church, but I soon learned they weren't just sleepy; they were comatose. A few weeks into that experience, I began to look around and I found a group of believers who several years earlier decided they would rather die a slow death than change, and no amount of passion or optimism by yet another in a parade of young, enthusiastic ministers was going to turn that church around.

On the surface, the church appeared to be another example of death by urban renewal and ethnic change. A decade or so earlier, the interstate came through town, forming an unnatural barrier between the church campus and downtown. More importantly, African American families slowly moved into the neighborhood and "white flight" took off like a jet on a short runway. Unlike other Anglo congregations, this one refused to sell out and move out, but, unfortunately, they also refused to open their hearts or their doors to their new neighbors. It *seemed* that the decline of that church could be tied unmistakably to the failure of the Anglos to embrace the influx of African Americans into the community, including the flight of the Anglos. By the time I arrived on the scene, few white families still lived in the vicinity, and almost all of them were elderly and unwilling to leave their homes of many, many years.

I said that on the surface the situation *appeared* to be the result of poor race relations, but I now understand that there was a more fundamental issue at work. The people of that church were convinced that church was about *them*. Their attitude was: *It's about us!* That's why they steadfastly refused to accept people of a different ethnicity. That's why they refused to reach out to their new neighbors. That's why they refused to follow the trend of moving the church to make it more attractive and convenient to the up-and-comers in their town. And that's why they died.

While I served that congregation, I presided over its funeral. Fortunately, it was not a drawn out, unnecessarily painful and agonizing death, but a relatively quick and surprisingly redemptive decision to remove life support. The leadership of the large church allowed me to work with the smaller group to make their own decision about whether to try to continue or to close their doors and allow members to seek other places of worship. Wisely, they decided to do the latter. The two Sunday School classes composed of elderly members moved as a group to the large church that had been supporting them for ten years. The handful of younger folk found other churches to join. They gave their property to the local Baptist Association, which served all of the Baptist congregations in that county, and a new Laotian congregation was started in the buildings. So the story has a happy ending, or at least happier than most.

I have begun this chapter with this story because in my mind it is a superb example of an attitude that hinders lifestyle compassion ministry. *The biggest barrier to lifestyle compassion ministry is a self-centered attitude.* That goes for churches and for individual believers. This is the attitude that says: It is about us.

I find that many church folk really do believe it's about them. They believe the church is there to serve them—to provide child care for their little ones, to educate their children in spiritual matters, to provide safe, so-attractive-that-their-teenagers-will-beg-to-come activities for their teens, to marry their young and bury their dead, to give them their weekly spiritual "fix" on Sundays, and so forth. And as long as this attitude prevails, there is little hope that many will develop lifestyle ministry, especially lifestyle compassion ministry for persons *outside* the church.

I am not the only church leader to come to this conclusion. Another is Reggie McNeal, who delivers a scathing critique of today's church in his book *The Present Future.* He proclaims an obvious truth: the church as we have known it is dying, and will pass from the scene if something doesn't change the church's focus. He says the church's internal focus is the primary cause of this fatal flaw:

Many congregations and church leaders, faced with the collapse of the church culture, have responded by adopting a refuge mentality. This is the perspective reflected in the approach to ministry that withdraws from the culture, that builds the walls higher and thicker, that tries to hang on to what we've got, that hunkers down to wait for the storm to blow over and for things to get back to "normal" so the church can resume its previous place in the culture. Those who hold this perspective frequently lament the loss of cultural support for church values and adopt an "us-them" dichotomous view of the world. Those with a refuge mentality view the world outside the church as the enemy. Their answer is to live inside the bubble in a Christian subculture complete with its own entertainment industry. Evangelism in this world-view is about churching the unchurched, not connecting people to Jesus. It focuses on cleaning people up, changing their behavior so Christians (translation: church people) can be more comfortable around them. Refuge Churches evidence enormous self-preoccupation. They deceive themselves into believing they are a potent force.[1]

McNeal reminds us that Jesus began a *movement*; he did not establish an *institution*. Yet, institutionalism has a firm grip on the church today, and its most effective tactic in maintaining its hold is the attitude that says it's about us. McNeal rightly observes:

> The target of most church ministry efforts has been on the church itself and church members. Just look at how the money is spent and what the church leadership spends time doing. We have already rehearsed the poor return on investment we are seeing for this focus.
>
> The church that wants to partner with God on his redemptive mission in the world has a very different target: the community. In the past if a church had any resources left over after staffing Sunday School, and so on, then it went to the community. In the future the church that "gets it" will staff to and spend its resources on strategies for community transformation. Members obviously have needs for pastoral care and spiritual growth. It is critical

that these be addressed. However, I am raising the question of how many church activities for the already-saved are justified when there are people who have never been touched with Jesus' love? The answer is a whole lot less than we've got going on now.[2]

It's Not Supposed to Be about Us

When Jesus began his public ministry, he did so in the familiar surroundings of his hometown synagogue. Luke tells us about it in the fourth chapter of his account of Jesus' life:

> He went to Nazareth, where he had been brought up, and on the Sabbath day he went into the synagogue, as was his custom. And he stood up to read. The scroll of the prophet Isaiah was handed to him. Unrolling it, he found the place where it is written:
>
> "The Spirit of the Lord is on me, because he has anointed me
>   to preach good news to the poor.
> He has sent me to proclaim freedom for the prisoners
>   and recovery of slight for the blind,
> to release the oppressed,
>   to proclaim the year of the Lord's favor."
>
> Then he rolled up the scroll, gave it back to the attendant and sat down. The eyes of everyone in the synagogue were fastened on him, and he said to them, "Today this scripture is fulfilled in your hearing." (Lk. 4:16–21)

This was not just Jesus taking his turn at reading Scripture in his home church. Nor was it his announcement in press conference fashion that he was that day launching his public ministry. It was nothing less than the platform for all he would do for the remainder of his public ministry. It was Jesus' mission statement. Everything he did from that moment until his death a few short years later can be traced back to these verses from Isaiah.

Look at what Jesus said he would do in his ministry. He would preach good news. To whom? The poor. Why did he (actually Isaiah) single out the poor? Because it is part of God's nature to sympathize with and be merciful toward the poor. (I say more

50   *The Samaritan Way*

about this in the next chapter.) The poor are not *us*. That is not
to say that there are no economically challenged persons in the
church. It is to say that Jesus' ministry was aimed at those who
perceived themselves to be *outsiders*, people such as Zacchaeus,
the woman at the well, and the woman who anointed and kissed
his feet.

In the Nazareth synagogue, Jesus said his ministry would
target people who had been marginalized by the world. How else
would you describe "prisoners," the "blind," and the "oppressed?"
They are hardly people who are among the respectable of
any community, especially in Jesus' day. They were not well
represented among the men in attendance the day Jesus read his
mission statement from Isaiah.

Jesus' ministry was not for those who merely came to fulfill
their religious duty in attending worship in Nazareth or in any
other synagogue; it was for those on the outside looking in. It was
not for any of the good people of Nazareth who occupied their
usual places in the synagogue that day, which is part of the reason
they reacted so violently to what he said. I don't think there is any
question that, at the outset, Jesus was the first to say that church is
not about us insofar as it is patterned after his ministry.

After his public ministry, Jesus spent a few weeks in intensive
training of the disciples, preparing them to carry on what he
began. That is my understanding of Acts 1:1: "In my former book,
Theophilus, I wrote about all that Jesus *began to do and to teach*"
(emphasis added). In the initial sentence of his record of the birth
and infancy of the church, Luke tells us that the Gospel account
given his name is just the first phase of the Kingdom issued in by
Jesus. In that first phase, Jesus was the doer and teacher. In the
second phase the church is the doer and teacher, and such doing
and teaching must be a continuation of "all that Jesus began to
do and to teach."

The importance of Acts 1, of course, is his farewell to the
disciples. In this goodbye that sounds more like a commissioning,
he reminds them of their mission: "You will receive power when
the Holy Spirit comes on you; and you will be my witnesses in
Jerusalem, and in all Judea and Samaria, and to the ends of the
earth" (Acts 1:8).

Clearly, it was Jesus' intention that his followers make him and his ministry known everywhere. "The ends of the earth" suggests that there is no part of the world, no people group, no race, no culture, no nation, no community, and no neighbor who is not of concern to the Father. If it had been Jesus' intent to build an exclusive group, we would be hard pressed to explain his commissioning in Acts 1:8. If he had merely wanted to form a collection of navel-gazers, we would not know what to do with this seminal verse. But we know that was not his intention and, therefore, that is not what the disciples-turned-apostles did and, furthermore, it is not what the church is about. In other words, church is not about us. Jesus said so. In perhaps the most succinct set of instructions he gave, he said his work is not about us, but about all the people *out there*.

Ed Stetzer and David Putman make just that point in their recent book, *Breaking the Missional Code*. Throughout their book, Stetzer and Putman hold high what they call the "missional church"—a church that is externally focused, in tune with the needs of the community and organized to meet those needs as much as possible. Interestingly, they say exactly what I am trying to say in this chapter. See if you agree.

> Missions makes this point: it is not about us and our preferences. It is about *his mission* and the fact that he sends us. We want to practice our preferences. We want things to be the way we like them. But God wants us to be on mission with him, to be sent to some group of people somewhere, and to minister in a way that meets their needs, not promotes our preferences. When we are functioning as God's church sent on mission, we will go into different cultures, contexts, and communities. We will proclaim a faithful gospel there in a culturally relevant way, and we will worship in a way that connects in that setting. When the connection is made, the code is broken. God does not tell us that we will always like it. He does say that we *always* need to function as his missionary church.[3]

I am laboring a bit over this point because it is so crucial to lifestyle compassion ministry. This comes right out of the very platform of Jesus' own ministry *and* his launching of the church into the world. For some of us this is so obvious as to be assumed. And yet it is not so obvious to many in today's church. It's not supposed to be about us, but, as the story I told at the start of this chapter suggests, *it actually is about us!*

We Have Seen the Enemy, and They Are Us

How come? If it is so clearly spelled out in Scripture and articulated by Jesus that his work is not about us, then how come so many of us think it is? Because we have created the expectation that churches are here to serve us. We have encouraged the consumer mentality that is pervasive in many churches. Milfred Minatrea comes to the same conclusion:

> Many Western churches are now focused mostly on sur-
> vival. These churches are no longer storming the gates
> of hell. They are simply trying to outlast the onslaught of
> secularism that threatens their existence. These churches
> are filled with members who have adopted and adapted
> to the consumer culture. Just as they count on Wal-Mart
> meeting their material needs, they expect their churches
> to provide religious goods and services. Many of their
> pastors...are struggling to hang on and give them access
> to a strong spiritual life.[4]

It starts with marketing. We appeal to selfish interests when we "market" our churches to the public. "Come to So-and-So Church: The place where your needs are met." Translation: "Church is a place where I can have it my way." Or, "Such-and-Such Church: Where everyone is number one!" Translation: "Church is a place where I can expect to be the center of attention."

We foster consumerism in our programming. We do our best to offer what people want, when they want it, and where they want it in the belief that if we give them what they want, they will come. And we *do* want them to come! A couple of years ago the church I served as pastor was trying to attract several young couples to become more involved in the church. Most of them had grown up in the church, gone off to college, and returned home to take jobs and settle down, but had not yet reestablished regular participation in worship or Bible study. Our ministry team talked about how we might draw these young folk back into the church and decided on a most traditional approach–start a Sunday School class just for them. We reasoned that they would not respond well to the invitation to be part of an established class, but one that was their own staffed with a teacher hand-picked to serve them would be irresistible. Lo and behold, it worked. They came...for a while. Then attendance in the class began to decline. The teacher, a well-educated, dedicated, mature Christian with at least one child the age of those in the class became concerned. Finally, she decided to get to the bottom of the drop-off in attendance. She ditched the lesson one Sunday and asked the members present what the problem was. She was told, I hope tactfully, that they did not enjoy her teaching style. They went on to tell her *who* they wanted for a teacher, a young man teaching elsewhere in Sunday School. Of course, she was stung by their response to her questions, but she was also wise and gracious enough to step aside. And guess who was asked to take the class? Now, even if he is a splendid teacher (and he is), and even if the class regains its former attendance pattern, and even if it grows numerically, it concerns me that we have told these young believers in a way they will not soon forget that *church is about them.* Any way you slice it, this attitude is a barrier to lifestyle compassion ministry.

American culture has huge influence on church life. By and large, Americans are highly individualistic, and, in more extreme cases, selfish. It is well known that our economic system has created a pervasive consumer mentality. The new ways marketers play to this mentality have become a unique form of entertainment in themselves. For example, you can go online and "design" your own car with just the features you want. It is now possible to customize sneakers over the Internet. There are fewer and fewer aspects of life not available to the have-it-your-way approach to marketing. Everything we want, we get–just as we like it.

People do not leave this way of thinking at home when they go to church. They expect options–in programming, in facilities, in churches. Church hopping is popular. It is driven by consu-merism–*what I want* is the trump card in my decision-making process. As one writer says: "Men's groups, ladies' groups, support groups, seniors' groups, pre-school mom's groups: they all play a part in advancing the organization by growing the customer base, and the customer base gladly plays along."[5] Another source rightly concludes: "Faith, like the buying of material goods, [is] a matter of individual choice and self-expression. And 'where religious affiliation is a matter of choice, religious organizations must compete for members and...the "invisible hand" of the marketplace is as unforgiving of ineffective religious firms as it is of their commercial counterparts.'"[6] This explains why corporate models, marketing strategies, and the like have become major players in ministry in American churches: We are in competition with other churches for survival. To appeal to religious consumers, we have to offer spiritual experiences and values in ways that appeal to them in the same way that a clothing designer markets his or her newest line of clothing. And this has the effect of making church folk think it's all about them. What chance does lifestyle compassion ministry that is driven by selflessness and is other-directed have in such an environment? Any church or individual believer who truly wants to pursue lifestyle compassion ministry will have to face these realities and deal with them before they see much movement toward Jesus-like ministry.

Even in cases in which people are giving significant chunks of their time and energy to help others, usually self-interest is somewhere close by. In the early '90s, Dr. Robert Wuthnow of Princeton University conducted a comprehensive study of Americans' views and experiences regarding compassion and acts of compassion. He found that most Americans "believe that we are driven by self-interest. In response to the question, 'On the whole, do you think people in our country are genuinely concerned about helping the needy, or are they mostly concerned about their own activities and interests?' only 24 percent of the people in [Wuthnow's] survey expressed confidence that there was a genuine concern for the needy; in comparison, 67 percent said people are concerned with their own activities and interests."[7]

After dissecting the data obtained in his survey of Americans regarding their thoughts about and involvement in compassion, and after reviewing the records of several in-depth interviews he conducted with persons many would say are models of compassion in terms of the amount of time they spend helping others, Wuthnow concludes that "the 'me society' stands in opposition to the 'we society.' Looking out for myself gets in the way of putting others first."[8] While Wuthnow was not examining believers' attitudes about lifestyle compassion ministry, his findings help explain why the church has a hard way to go in leading her members to give themselves to a lifestyle of serving others. You could argue that believers do not necessarily think like the rest of the population, that they are driven by more selfless motives, but statistics indicate you would be wrong. Every study I have seen says that church folk are not different from others in what they think and how they live, except for maybe where they spend their Sunday mornings.

Another contributing factor in the inward focus of many churches is the concept of membership. Membership in itself is not a bad thing. When I was a pastor, I always challenged persons to join the church they attended, which was usually mine. However, in a few cases, when people who attended my church regularly for a long period of time but declined to join, I suggested that it might be better for them to locate a church they could join. In my mind it's all about commitment, which is totally consistent with the ministry of Jesus, although he knew nothing of the contemporary concept of church membership.

Yet membership becomes part of the problem of consumerism in the church when it causes church folk to distinguish between themselves and nonmembers. As missional leader Mark Thames, says: "Most people today 'hold membership' in stores such as Blockbuster Video or Sam's Club. Inevitably, people bring their idea of membership to the church rather than carry the church's idea of membership into the world... Members, the people on the inside, do as little as is required to be part and have the benefit. Non-members, those on the outside, do as much as required to share the benefit without becoming a member."[9]

At its worst, the idea of membership feeds the "it's about us" mentality. Church members sometimes harbor the attitude that since *they* are members and *they* support the church financially and with their presence, *they* should be given priority in the ministries of the church. The consequence of this attitude is the neglect, either implicitly or outright, of people who are not members of the church. When the last church I served as pastor was debating what to do about worship—whether to have two services of different kinds or one—a member approached me following one of our congregational meetings on this issue. She was almost in tears expressing her disappointment that she could no longer worship with her entire family because her now-grown children preferred the contemporary service, while she and her husband attended the traditional worship service. This was extremely important to her. She said she had no problem with the church trying to reach unchurched people—the stated reason for beginning a contemporary service. She just didn't see why it had to interfere with her family's being together. This woman was inconsistent and she did not realize it. Her members-first thinking blinded her to the discrepancy.

I have known of cases in which church members behave and talk as if they were country club members—expecting certain services and treatment, a particular type of relationship (i.e., respectful, polite, but not too close for fear that the minister will know too much) with the "hired help" (the pastor and staff), and so forth as a result of their membership in the church. One of the most revealing examples of this attitude is the comment a church member made to a pastor following a worship service. As he shook the minister's hand at the church door on his way out of the sanctuary, he said, "That wasn't a thousand dollar sermon," suggesting that he didn't get his money's worth for his offering that day, as if the offering were an entertainment fee.

Here is another story that exposes the members-first or "it's about us" attitude. Years ago, a newly appointed parish finance chairman began his term by reviewing all the church's expenses—from pencils to vestments. One item sent him into a case of near apoplexy. The church had an old Coke machine in the basement. While Cokes cost anywhere from 50 cents to a dollar everywhere else in town, this old machine still doled out bottles of Coca-Cola for 10 cents. The parish was losing a fortune on keeping the machine stocked with bargain Cokes. The finance chairman was adamant: the machine had to go. The parish council agreed and the machine was unplugged and stored away.

What the parish soon discovered was that their Coke machine was the busiest machine in town. Thirsty salespeople and shoppers from the plaza across the street would drop by for an ice-cold Coke. Kids of all ages would grab a Coke on their way home from school. On Sundays most of the young people of the parish would have an informal social hour around the machine after

Mass. The choir and the many parish committees and ministry groups who would meet and work in the church would drink the machine dry every week.

At its next meeting, the council was presented with several petitions to return the machine. The first came from the senior high youth group. At the top of their petition they quoted Matthew 25:35: "I was thirsty and you gave me a drink" (paraphrase). The kids pointed out that the Coke machine was a form of Christian hospitality, that it encouraged community, that it welcomed strangers, that it was a form of outreach to the neighborhood. The antiquated Coke machine was returned to the parish basement, where it remains to this day, doling out Cokes for a dime.[10] Whereas this story has a happy ending, many do not. The self-centered thinking of inwardly focused churches more often than not prevails.

God's Mirrors

Most of what I have said in this chapter has to do with the way congregations see the purpose of the church—to serve *them*. But it is merely an extension of individuals' thinking. The way to change the way congregations think is to change the way individual believers think.

Max Lucado has written a splendid little book, *It's Not About Me*.[11] Lucado rightly says being followers of Jesus means life is no longer about us; it's about "Him." In chapter after chapter he challenges us to replace our "it's about me" thinking with "it's about Him" thinking.

I find one of his chapters especially compelling. He says we are God's mirrors. Our job, our calling, is to reflect the glory of God. He cites 2 Corinthians 3:18: "And we, with our unveiled faces reflecting like mirrors the brightness of the Lord, all grow brighter and brighter as we are turned into the image that we reflect..." (Jerusalem Bible). He says we are like the moon, a sphere of mass without a light of our own, but lighted and useful for humans millions of miles away when we reflect the Son's light.

This is what I am trying to say in this chapter. It's not about us, never was and never will be. And no matter how much we try to make it so, it can never be. To see ourselves as God's mirrors is to adjust our thinking. It is to reposition ourselves in such a way as to become useful to the self-giving God.

A Poignant Parable

Several years ago a friend gave me a copy of a contemporary parable, which I have used on several occasions. Better than anything I have come across, this story exposes the "it's about us" attitude in today's church.

On a certain stretch of rugged seacoast there was once a small rescue station. Although its headquarters was a weather-beaten, old beach house, and its equipment was meager—it had only one battered lifeboat—its team of volunteer members tirelessly scanned the seas and went out day and night in search of those lost in the shipwrecks that frequently occurred in those waters. Many lives were saved by the heroic work of this little station, and its fame spread. Many of those rescued, and numbers of others who admired this work, wanted to become members of this life-saving team and lend their time, effort and money to its cause. They felt the station should have larger, more adequate facilities as the first refuge for those rescued from the sea. A beautiful and elaborate building was erected. The old emergency cots were replaced with comfortable, soft beds. Several new lifeboats were purchased, and a staff of professional life-saving specialists was hired to staff and direct the work. This little life-rescuing station grew rapidly. By this time, fewer and fewer members were going out in life-saving expeditions. They now spent more of their time in the station building, which they used as a sort of club. They decorated every room exquisitely, and held wonderful parties and weekly meetings. They were careful, however, to retain a symbolic lifeboat in the room where they inducted new members.

About this time a large ship was wrecked in a storm, and sank off the coast near the station. The hired, professional crew worked feverishly through the night, bringing in boatload after boatload of wet, chilled, dirty, and half-drowned people. Some of them belonged to ethnic minorities, and all of them were sick, sick from the trauma of the night. The beautiful new clubhouse was considerably messed up. The next week the property committee of the station installed an outdoor shower where shipwrecked victims could be cleaned up before being brought inside the building. And, at the next business meeting things came to a head. A resolution was presented that the club should dispense with its life-saving activities, because they were disruptive to the fellowship of the club. A few members objected that, after all, life-rescuing was the purpose for establishing the station in the beginning and they were still called a life-saving station. But they were voted down and told that if they wanted to save all the kinds of people who were being shipwrecked in those waters, they could move down the coast and start their own life-saving station.

And that's what they did. But, strangely enough, history repeated itself. The second station followed the course of the first. And a third began only to succumb to the same fate. Today you can find a number of exclusive clubs all along that stretch of seacoast. There are still frequent shipwrecks in the rough waters along that coast, but most of the people drown.

Notes

[1]Reggie McNeal, *The Present Future: Six Tough Questions for the Church* (San Francisco: Jossey-Bass, 2003), 8–9.

[2]Ibid., 32.

[3]Ed Stetzer and David Putman, *Breaking the Missional Code: Your Church Can Become a Missionary in Your Community* (Nashville: Broadman & Holman, 2006), 32.

[4]Milfred Minatrea, *Shaped by God's Heart: The Passion and Practices of Missional Churches* (San Francisco: Jossey-Bass, 2004), 7.

[5]Titus Benton, "Is Consumerism Killing the Church?" *Relevant Magazine*, posted on the Internet at www.relevantmagazine.com.

[6]Skye Jethani, "Leader's Insight: From Christ's Church to iChurch," posted on the Internet at www.christianitytoday.com.

[7]Robert Wuthnow, *Acts of Compassion: Caring for Others and Helping Ourselves* (Princeton, N.J.: Princeton University Press, 1991), 19.

[8]Ibid., 21.

[9]Quoted in Minatrea, *Shaped by God's Heart,* 32.

[10]"Seventh Sunday of Easter," *Connections: The Newsletter of Ideas, Resources and Information for Homilists and Preachers* (Londonderry, N.H.: Media Works, May 1999), 2–3.

[11]Max Lucado, *It's Not About Me* (Nashville: Integrity Publishers, 2004).

4

It's about Them

Brethren, let us heartily love all whom Jesus loves. Cherish the tired and suffering.
   Visit the fatherless and the widow. Care for the faint and the feeble.
   Bear with the melancholy and despondent.

CHARLES H. SPURGEON

Some time ago I had a promotional video made for Operation Inasmuch, in which participants in this model of community ministry in the city where I lived tell what it has meant to them and what they hope to accomplish through that one day of community ministry. The video concludes with a young boy, perhaps eight years old, saying on camera: "I just like helping God out and make it easier for people. *It's not about us; it's about them.*" When editing the video, I deliberately chose to close it with the boy's statement, in part because it is a child talking and that is always more persuasive, but primarily because his last line is what I want to have ringing in the ears of those who watch the video. If the line resonates with them, then they will embrace the Operation Inasmuch model of community ministry.

   In the previous chapter, I expounded on the first part of that line—"it's not about us." Hopefully, an adequate case was made for the misplaced priorities that dominate so many congregations today. Internal focus is a powerful disease of epidemic proportions in American churches today. Until this disease is diagnosed, it is unlikely that congregations will break free from the grip of institutionalism and reclaim the vision of Jesus as set forth in Luke 4. But is not enough simply to expose the problem. A new focus needs to supplant the old one. If all we do is acknowledge that we have made church about us, that may awaken us to a reality that will help us get better, but sooner or later we have to put in place a new focus or new priorities. The person who struggles with obesity has to do more than admit he is overweight. That is a reasonable beginning, but he will soon have to follow that admission with a new lifestyle that includes better eating habits and exercise.

In his excellent book *Encounter God in the City,* Randy White reminds us, "All true and deep change involves both a turning away from something and turning toward something else. It involves a rejection and embrace."[1] All of this is to say that we now turn our attention to *them,* the "*them*" to whom that eight-year-old boy was referring at the end of the video described above.

I am convinced this is where "the rubber hits the road" in lifestyle compassion ministry. Let's be honest. For most church folk taking up a lifestyle of compassion ministry will be a huge change—not just in how they spend their time, but in how they think and feel, and what they allow to move them. And the most effective way to help believers shift their values from matters of self-interest to people in need is to help them see those people.

Go back to the model of the Samaritan in the timeless story Jesus gave in Luke 10. As stated in chapter 2, what separated him from those who went before him was that he actually saw the victim wounded and bleeding by the side of the road. He saw the man through eyes of compassion, and the victim's needs superseded anything else the Samaritan had on his agenda that day. Using that scenario, I ask you to consider victims who need our ministry today.

Victims of Homelessness

John Mitchell rises for work with a siren blaring inside a homeless shelter in Harlem—a signal for the nearly 200 residents to line up for twice-a-week drug tests. A 47-year-old former crack addict, Mitchell says he was in and out of prison or homeless for more than 20 years, robbing people for drug money and digging through trash cans for food. "I was that type of guy that, guess what, you didn't want to see on the streets," Mitchell says. "I came to the conclusion [that] this time around I learned what that word *surrender* means."

Seven months ago, the father of two teens became sober and entered the city's "Ready, Willing & Able" program that provides shelter (10 men to a room), hot meals and a job cleaning the streets that pays up to $7 an hour. Mitchell's infectious laugh and ready quips make him the unofficial leader of the crew working the West Side this morning. He sweeps the streets and dumps garbage cans, the steady rain dripping off his nose.

His mind is on the future—he's studying at night to be a nurse's aide. "I gotta keep saying, this is not going to last forever, there's a bigger picture," he says. "It's like riding a bike...right now I'm using training wheels. Before I know it, I'll be popping a wheelie."[2]

This is one of the more encouraging stories of the hundreds of thousands of people who are homeless in America. He is actually moving toward independence and there is reason to believe he has made it by now (this story ran in 2005). Unfortunately, he is the exception. Homelessness is one of the more formidable forces victimizing people the world over. The National Alliance to End Homelessness published a book—*Homelessness Counts*—in 2006. It includes the following stats[3]:

- 744,313 people were identified as homeless in January 2005
- 56 percent of homeless people counted were living in shelters and transitional housing and, shockingly, 44 percent were unsheltered.
- 59 percent of homeless people counted were single adults and 41 percent were persons living in families.
- In total, 98,452 homeless families were counted.
- 23 percent of homeless people were reported as chronically homeless, which, according to HUD's definition, means that they are homeless for long periods or repeatedly.

Statistics help us grasp the scope of homelessness, but they do little to move us toward ministering to homeless persons. For that to happen, *we have to* see *them.* Ideally, you would put this book down, get in your car, and drive to the nearest shelter for homeless persons. You would spend enough time there to learn how many people stay there each night, what some of their stories are, and what the shelter is doing to care for them. If that doesn't move you toward doing what you can to minister to them, it is highly unlikely anything I say in this book will do it either. however, since I have your attention, let me try to put a face on homelessness for you.

Chicago, 8:30 AM

A 10-degree wind chill whips through the North Side streets of Chicago as 6-year-old Angelina Torres, in her pink wool hat, and her twin, Angel, in his Spiderman gloves, make their way to kindergarten. Their mom, Eileen Rivera, leads the way on the seven-block walk. Her two older sons, Omar, 9, and JJ, 10, have already left—a bus picked them up at 8 a.m. at the Sylvia Center, the shelter where the family has lived for eight months. Her arms folded against the cold, Rivera walks briskly, noting her twins have stayed in shelters about half their lives. "They just blend right in," She pauses, then adds: "It's sad."

Her husband, Jesús Torres, recently found work operating a forklift, earning $7 an hour. The husky, outgoing father has been a handyman, pizza deliveryman, ice cream cart driver, cashier and drug store clerk—sometimes working in exchange for welfare checks. The Torreses are on waiting lists for public and subsidized housing. Rivera tells her children this is just a steppingstone. "Guys," she says, "we have to do this just a little longer. We have to go through this to get to the shining star."

Rivera knows exactly what that will be: "Your own toilet. Your own tissues. Your own bath. Your own window. Things that are yours. Just yours."

With the school day over, Eileen Rivera's four kids are home; the boys watch cartoons, Angela plays with Barbie dolls. Rivera, 38, slips off her long-haired dark wig—a stress-related illness has left her bald—and sits on a bed in the vault-like room. "Sometimes," she says, "I feel like saying to someone, 'Give my kids a home. Just a taste of it. For a bit.'"

After the apartment building they lived in burned down in 1998, they lost their home; Rivera's husband, who was a handyman there, also lost his job. They moved to his mother's home in Puerto Rico but eventually returned to Chicago. Now Rivera knows the written rules to shelter life—and the unwritten ones. "My kids already know we've got to make friends. We can't make enemies," she says.

Though they have little space, the Torreses proudly save every "student of the month" certificate, every blue ribbon their kids win. Jesús Torres, 43, also keeps a letter he wrote to social service officials, "I want permanent and stable housing for me and my family," it says. "I want to... take responsibility as the head of the household. I want to be a productive member of society."

Torres is saving money. The shelter requires residents to set aside 75 percent of their earnings. He pays $43 monthly to store his family's belongings until they find a home. He's an optimist. His wife tries to be. "Sometimes I feel like it's not going to come and I'm just fooling myself," she says. "My kids will see me sad and say, 'You said we were going to get a home.'... They make me feel like there is hope."[4]

Nicole Hudson has a roof over her head—for now. Sitting in Covenant House, a shelter for homeless and runaway teens, she ticks off the places she has lived in her 20 years: eight foster homes, two group homes, two shelters, one transitional apartment. She's also stayed with her mother three times and her grandparents twice. This is Hudson's fourth stint at Covenant House. She has been kicked out three times for breaking the rules.

She's been on the streets three times in the past year, living on-and-off with 25 other teens in a narrow alley off Hollywood Boulevard [in Hollywood, Calif.]. "It's just horrible," she says in a husky voice with a hint of a Southern drawl. "We don't even like to walk past older people on the street and see them still sleeping all wrapped up in stinky blankets, dirty mattresses, their hair not combed. What happened to the blue skies, you know, and the sun-shining days when you were little? It's like the world just crashes when you get older and your mind comes to reality."[5]

A few blocks from downtown Las Vegas's casinos, Clarence Woods is on his way to buy a pack of cigarettes. A week ago, he lived on the streets, but work as a day laborer has allowed him to move into a $370-a-month hotel. He doesn't know how long his luck will hold. The 53-year-old Woods is a father of five but says he is too embarrassed to tell his children where he's living. He says he ended up homeless because he was irresponsible. "It's like hell," he says, his cranberry stocking hat pulled snug over his ears in the desert chill. Woods says there aren't places to help homeless people like him. He once did well in Las Vegas and owned his own upholstery shop, he says. But he went bankrupt and ended up without a home. He calls himself a recreational drug user, drinker, and gambler. "It's a real trap," he says, the neon signs flashing behind him, "but it's what Las Vegas is all about."[6]

Homelessness has left the road strewn with bodies. Can you see them? Like the victim in the parable of the Good Samaritan, these bodies are alive but only barely. Mental illness, addiction, or unemployment have brutalized people and left them "on the road."

Victims of Poverty

Poverty is a bully whose turf is the whole world. The nameless victim in the story of the Good Samaritan was attacked and beaten severely by thieves and left for dead. Was he beaten because he resisted? When the robbers demanded his money, did he fight them and lose? Or was he beaten first and robbed after he was subdued? We will never know. These are details that Jesus considered irrelevant to his reason for telling the story. Poverty is every bit as brutal as those who brutalized the victim in Jesus' story.

Poverty is more than the lack of material things or money. It is a culture of powerlessness. It is more than insufficient funds with which to provide for oneself and one's family. It is a system of injustice and oppression and hopelessness. For those in poverty, whatever the causes, it is like a cage or prison from which there is no escape.

Most of my readers are not poor...by any definition. Therefore, most of us (including myself, as a middle-class American) do not understand poverty. And while I am not naïve enough to think that a few pages here will get us all "up to speed" on this issue, it is necessary to offer some definition of poverty to provide, if for no other reason, a frame of reference. *Wikipedia* describes poverty as "Material need, typically including the necessities of daily living (food, clothing, shelter, and health care)...a condition in which a person or community is deprived of, and/or lacks the essentials for a minimum standard of well-being and life. These essentials may be material resources such as food, safe drinking water, and shelter, or they may be social resources such as access to information, education, health care, social status, political power, or the opportunity to develop meaningful connections with other people in society."[7]

The World Bank conducted research among 20,000 poor people in twenty-three countries, identifying several common factors contributing to poverty:

- Precarious livelihoods
- Excluded locations
- Physical limitations
- Gender relationships
- Problems in social relationships
- Lack of security
- Abuse by those in power
- Disempowering institutions
- Limited capabilities
- Weak community organizations

Did you notice how many of these factors are external to individuals' own behavior, choices, or capacities? The vast majority of poor people in the world were born there. They did not make a wrong turn somewhere and end up in poverty as if they misread the directions to the good life. Some did. Some have made such poor choices and they are suffering dire consequences. But most have not. They have never known anything else. Whether in Appalachia or the urban ghettos in the United States, whether in the war-torn countries of Africa or in the slums of Southeast Asia, poverty is the only life millions of people in this world know.

Poverty is so pervasive and victimizes so many people that we cannot consider it as a single category of "need." To do it justice, we have to break it down into several categories: children in poverty, the working poor, and the elderly poor.

Children in Poverty

The National Center for Children in Poverty reports that 13 million children in the United States live in families with incomes below the federal poverty level, which is $20,000 a year for a family of four. "The number of children living in poverty increased by more than 11 percent between 2000 and 2005. There are 1.3 million more children living in poverty today than in 2000, despite indications of economic recovery and growth."[8] As alarming as these figures are, the real situation is actually much worse. Research shows consistently that families actually need about twice the federal poverty level to make ends meet. Thirty-nine percent of America's children—more than 28 million—live in families below this level.

The picture is uglier for minority children. Thirty-five percent of African American children, 28 percent of Latino/a children, and 29 percent of Native American children live in poor families, compared to 10 percent of white children. Children in immigrant families are far more likely to live in poor families. The economic hardships of children are staggering.

- 16 percent of households with children experience food insecurity.
- 41 percent of families who rent their homes spend more than a third of their income on rent.

Compared to white families with children, African American and Latino/a families with children are more than twice as likely to experience economic hardships.[9]

Again, statistics inform but do not motivate. They are as likely to demotivate, overwhelming us to the point of paralysis. When you read the statistics shown above, does it make you want to volunteer at an agency to help poor children, or does it cause you to ask: "How can we make any difference at all in this problem?" Stories, however, can motivate and lead to transformation. Here are a couple of stories of children in poverty.

Jessie Staley is a teenager living in Harts, West Virginia. Like any other teenager, she dreams of going to the prom and graduating form high school. However, while her friends buy prom dresses, she struggles to feed her sisters and brothers. Other families in her town choose among colleges for their children, Jessie's chooses between medical care and welfare.

As many of her friends live as carefree adolescents, Jessie assumes the role of caretaker in her family. She is the oldest of three children and, in the absence of a mother, she is responsible to do for them what most parents do. Her father ekes out a living as a truck driver, but his twelve-to-fifteen-hour shifts don't provide enough income to pay the bills. Although the family is not homeless, they have only $120 each month to buy food. Often there isn't enough to last the month, so Jessie turns to charities in her community. Her family constantly struggles to make ends meet. For example, choosing inexpensive over healthy foods has hurt the family's health. Jessie's Dad has a heart condition and struggles against obesity–the result of eating too much high fat, processed foods that so frequently make up a low-income diet.

Jessie's day begins early, after her father leaves for work. She wakes up her brother and sister, feeds them, and sends them to school. After attending classes all day, she prepares dinner, helps her siblings with class assignments, and puts them to bed–all before starting her own homework. Her dream of going to college is clouded by fears that her father will need for her to remain close by to help with the family after graduation.

An official with a group that works with poor rural communities said that the issue for kids like Jessie is not just money, but a lack of social service organizations in rural areas and a lack of opportunities for young people to create networks for success. Such young people usually lack the money or resources to build a different way of life.

Poverty has left children by the side of the road in every community. Can you see them? When it comes to being authentic followers of Jesus, it's not about us, *it's about them*.

The Working Poor

A common assumption about poor folk by "nonpoor" folk is that they are unemployed either because they are unemployable (i.e., disabled or without skills) or because they choose not to work. The assumption is that employment is the surest prevention for poverty. Not so—or, rather, I should say: absolutely not so! Although it is a little dated, Timothy Keller in his book *Ministries of Mercy* says:

> Approximately one-third of the poor are children. Another third are adults who are working, but not making a wage that lifts them out of poverty. A sixth consist of the elderly and the mentally or physically disabled. Only the final sixth consist of the "controversial" people—single parents home with children, and persons who are able-bodied but not working.[10]

Nearly 40 percent of working-age poor people are employed, and the percentage working full-time all year increased 45 percent during the period from 1978 to 2002.[11] Philip Coltoff, chief executive of Children's Aid Society, says: "This is a very interesting sociological change. We've created a new class of poor. There is this huge group of people who want to work, who are working, but it's a form of being indentured. America has always been built on the belief that you can do better, but we have shut down the ladder to the middle class."[12]

These are our neighbors whose lives are turned upside down with an extended illness or a major repair job to their home or car. They are eking out a living with no margins for unexpected expenses, and when those crises come, these folk are often forced to leave their homes or fall behind on paying some of the essential bills. Or they choose not to make repairs to their home, so that their living conditions deteriorate over time. The working poor are people often overlooked by the systems in our communities designed to help people in need. Their needs are judged not to be sufficiently urgent to warrant response and so they go unmet.

Some of the working poor are in our churches. I remember hearing Lisbeth, a friend and member of one church I served, tell her story. She is bright, talented, and resourceful. She is a single mother with a couple of part-time jobs, so she is employed. However, her income is not sufficient to allow any breathing room for emergencies. Several years ago she needed work done on her home but couldn't afford to have it done. She entertained to thought of trying to do the work herself, but soon took a more realistic approach—wait until she could get help. When our church did an Operation Inasmuch, a crew of church members identified her home as one to receive some repairs. Years later, she still glows when she talks about fellow church members coming to her home and doing for her what she could not do.[13]

The working poor are people like Freda Lee, 33, who has two jobs—as a marketer and a cashier. She goes to the Loaves and Fishes Ministry—ironically flanked by McDonald's and Burger King—to receive food for herself and her three sons. "America is meant to be free. What's free?" she laughs. "All we can do is pay off the basics."[14]

Sherry Byrum, 48, feels there is no way up. She lives in Spokane, Washington, works full-time at a day care center earning almost $9 an hour, and earns $8.43 an hour providing home care for a disabled girl on the side. Health insurance costs her $71 a week. Her work is fulfilling. "When a child gives you a hug or draws you a little picture, it means everything." But it's financially frustrating. Her husband just had open-heart surgery and doesn't work, so she brings in the only income. They live in a thirty-year-old mobile home and get their groceries at the local food bank. They also have medical costs because both are diabetic. "Last week, we went several days without really eating. We've got to pay our bills," she says. "I can't buy the things I should eat because of the diabetes. There are some times I go to bed in tears thinking I just can't do it all."[15]

So what's the culprit here? Is it poverty, or an economic system that is stacked against millions of people? The answer is: *yes.* Some of the people in need by the Jericho Road are the working poor. They work. They receive wages, but not enough to take care of them or to protect them from expensive emergencies. Can you see them? They may not appear as desperate as others we have considered, and by comparison they aren't, but they are people in need. They need for us to see them. They are part of the "*them*" we mean when we say: it's not about us; it's about *them.*

The Elderly Poor

Another group victimized by poverty is the elderly. They have passed the wage-earning years. Their income and resources are limited in most cases, and hardly keep up with inflation. Many have not been able to plan for retirement, depending solely on Social Security. Speaking of Social Security, it is responsible for keeping millions of seniors off the poverty rolls, but that is merely a statistical construct. The reality is that millions of people hover just barely above that controversial line and daily face decisions as to how best to use their meager resources—to buy medicines, purchase food, or pay the rent. Says David Callahan in his online article, "Still with Us: Elderly Poverty in America":

> One of the greatest successes of American social policy over the last few decades has been a dramatic reduction in poverty among the elderly. Even so, some 3.3 million seniors still live below the poverty line. Several million more scrape by just above the poverty line. For many of these people, poverty is the reward for adult lives spent continuously in the workforce or raising children and managing a family. Good housing and proper medical care are often out of reach for the poor elderly, or so expensive that little money is left over for other needs. Hundreds of thousands of elders go hungry every month.[16]

Older women are particularly vulnerable to the inadequacies of our systems. Many elderly women married in the 1940s and '50s did not work for pay, but rather reared children and supported their husbands. Therefore, "for many elderly women, poverty begins when married life ends. The vast majority of widows in poverty become poor only after their husbands die."[17]

I would not rate my experience with community ministry as valid research on this issue. However, I can say that most of the home repair projects in which I have been involved—a couple of dozen in about twenty years—have been for elderly residents. In all of these cases the residents were required to meet low-income requirements before they qualified for the projects on their homes. They were not poor by some standards, but their resources were insufficient to make the necessary repairs on their home, which is why my church friends and I helped them.

My most recent experience was in East Tennessee, where I now live. I worked all day repainting the interior of a widow's home. She had lived in the home for over twenty years. All of the walls and ceilings were a dingy gray from years of heating the home with kerosene heaters. A local agency "scoped out" the project and provided the paint. The volunteers had the joy of spending a day in this woman's home transforming it in a single day. I do not know if her income was below or above the federal poverty line. But I do know that her home badly needed painting and we were able to help her. She is part of the "*them*" we mean when we say: it's not about us; it's about *them*. Can you see the elderly poor?

While writing this chapter, I Googled "elderly poor" and ran across an interesting posting on Craig's List, an Internet-based sort of swap-shop. It was posted three days before I wrote this chapter. It said: "My neighbor is elderly, been ill of late and cannot afford to buy a furnace for her home. She spent half of last winter huddled next to a space heater after the furnace died. The house has steam radiators and the former furnace burned natural gas. If anyone has a furnace used or otherwise to donate, I would be very grateful and will arrange to have it picked up."[18] Now, there is a true neighbor! If more of us were this kind of neighbor, perhaps there would be no need for a book calling all believers to lifestyle compassion ministry.

Victims of Disease

Lifestyle compassion ministry targets the basic needs of people, and no need is more basic than health. For all our advancements in medicine, disease is still as potent an enemy of shalom as ever. Its victims are all along the highway of life in every community. Young, old, poor, middle-class, men, women, children—no one is beyond the reach of disease. Sickness is a universal need and produces people in need by the hordes. When we consider the persons who need our lifestyle of compassion ministry, we dare not exclude the sick.

By "the sick," I mean not only the hundreds of people occupying the hospital rooms in your community, but the many,

many others who are home but not well. I mean the disabled, both physically and mentally. As I write this, I am thinking of a friend who has a ministry to the residents in a group home near my home. As far as I know, no one "recruited" my friend to do this ministry. She initiated it out of her own sense of compassion. The residents in the home are not physically ill; they are mentally ill and have nowhere to live. The group home provides a bed, bath, and three meals a day. There are few organized activities for them and, to be honest, there are not many activities they can participate in. My friend goes there every month to share with them. She puts on a birthday party for any residents who have a birthday that month.

I have been honored to accompany her at Christmas. She purchases a small box of toiletries, snacks, and one or two very small gifts for each resident. She prepares a simple snack of fruit, cookies, and punch for them. We sing Christmas carols and I read the Christmas story from the Bible. (I usually read about the announcement of Jesus' birth to the shepherds because they represent God's priority of the disadvantaged and marginalized.) Then my friend gives out the presents to the residents. Most of them open their gifts and are very pleased with them even though they are pretty much the same items every year. Some of the residents choose not to open their gifts right away but wait until they can do so privately. As you can see in reading this, my friend has taught me much about seeing these victims by the side of the road and stopping to minister to them.

When illness attacks, its victims are not only the individuals who become sick but also their families. The sick person's loved ones are often impacted more than the individual. Hospital waiting rooms are subcultures of pain. Anxiety, fear, and loneliness take a heavy toll on family members who spend long hours and, sometimes, days clinging to threads of hope. If we could see the emotional strain such folk experience, they would appear every bit as battered and beaten as the victim in Jesus' parable. But emotional pain is hard to see, so we look past it. We walk past it.

Not Marie. When her church did Operation Inasmuch the first time, she agreed to be the project leader for the Hospital Waiting Room Project. Her team prepared baskets of snacks and toiletries and delivered them to Park West Hospital special unit lounges. The baskets contain microwavable items, crackers, cookies, mouthwash, toothpaste, toothbrushes, and items for children. Marie and her friends attached a card to each of the baskets, simply stating that they came from her church and gave the church's name, address, phone number and Web site. In delivering the each basket, they said: "We brought this basket for you to enjoy and hope it's a blessing to you."

The baskets were so well received that Marie has continued to provide the basket ministry to the hospital lounges. The recipients warmly thanked Marie and her friends for providing them and Marie saw how needed the baskets and visits were. Shortly after this foray into the sad environment of illness, the hospital contacted Marie and asked if she would consider bringing baskets again. Since then, she has gone once a month to continue this ministry. She says, "I am so proud to get to deliver the baskets, because I know how much good they do and I know God gets the glory for it." Marie is one of many who have discovered their own, personal ministries, in part because she ventured out in a one-day Operation Inasmuch and in part because she went with eyes wide open and, like the Samaritan, refused to pass by the people she met in need, but rather stopped to help them.

Prisoners

Victims? Are prisoners also victims? They aren't, at least not in the usual sense. They victimized others. They have been convicted of stealing, robbing, assaulting, or murdering innocent people. Yet they are victims in many cases, victims of circumstances, neglect, or abuse. I met a young man I will call Sam. He is in his early twenties. His father abused him and his siblings, inciting in him the kind of anger that runs deep and long, the kind of anger that eventually leads to trouble. Sure enough, he ran afoul of the law and spent years in a juvenile detention facility. His siblings were placed in foster homes. Hopefully, they found the nurture and love they needed to recover from their emotional wounds. But Sam didn't. Because he was the oldest, he suffered worse abuse than his siblings and will likely spend the rest of his life dealing with the effects of that abuse. When he deals with it in healthy ways, he does well. When his anger gets the best of him, he becomes destructive. He is currently living in subsidized housing. He has no job and no prospects for one—few employers want to hire a young man with a record. He has no transportation so his options are limited. Sam is, or has been, a prisoner but he is a victim nonetheless.

Here is another prisoner's story, told in a letter from a prisoner who receives ministry through Chuck Colson's Prison Fellowship:

> I'd like to tell you about my past. I was born into a family of [five siblings] in Colorado. We were very poor. My father was a drunk and an addict. My mother was hardly around, and she would never stand up to my father. When I was four, he held our family hostage for eight hours using a shotgun. I still feel fear from that night. Father went to prison and life got worse, so I started taking care of myself and the family. By age seven I was robbing homes and stealing food, clothes, cars—anything we needed at home. When dad got out on parole, I began selling drugs for him. [Soon after] I was taken to foster care for neglect. After years of abuse, DSS finally wanted to claim neglect. It made me rage inside. I ran away, back home. This [cycle continued] each time with the same result—running back home.
>
> In the ninth grade I was arrested for three counts of burglary and sentenced to five years as a juvenile offender, six as a youthful offender, 12 years suspended, two years county jail, two years community corrections, and four years probation—a total of 31 years. When I transferred to Lookout Mountain, Colorado, I earned my GED and several trades: screen printing, janitorial skills, horticulture, construction, residential wiring, and a lot about computers. After a reconsideration hearing I transferred again and started college classes. Then the most important thing happened. My professor, a graduate of Harvard Law School, reviewed my case. He [showed me in the law] that I was not eligible to be sentenced as an adult. The DA is trying to say they sentenced me correctly.
>
> My life is a mess right now, but I have one sure thing in my life—God. He has forgiven me for all I have done. Through His Son's blood my slate is clean. He said so in the Bible in John 3:16, Matthew 6:33, and 1 John 1:9. The whole reason I wrote this is to show that if I can believe

in Jesus after a life like mine, anyone can believe and be saved.[19]

God is calling people to be in ministry with prisoners. Chuck Colson's journey is well known. After decades of ministry following his own experience in prison, he has become a model of redemption through lifestyle compassion ministry to prisoners.

Steve Humphreys is another example of lifestyle ministry. He ministers to the imprisoned. He leads Focus Prison Ministries, headquartered in Knoxville, Tennessee. He left a successful career as a CPA to launch this Christian ministry to some of our society's most overlooked people–prisoners. It began when he felt God was telling him to visit a relative (actually his wife's relative) who was doing time as a convicted double murderer. This occurred while he was in the process of working his way through the popular discipleship study *Experiencing God.* He felt God was telling him that he should visit his relative, who by this time had been in prison several years with almost no contact from his family. At first Steve did not act on the spiritual notion of visiting a convicted felon, relative or not. His wife strongly discouraged him from going. But he came to a point in his study that he knew he would never know God's will for him if he did not obey what God was telling him to do, including visiting the incarcerated relative.

By his own description, Steve felt no compassion for prisoners. His attitude was that they had done the crime, so they should have to do the time. Convicted prisoners did not deserve his compassion. But when he visited his relative, what he saw changed his heart. He saw men with children on their laps, surrounded by family members, just ordinary men who happened to be dressed in striped uniforms.   The eyes of his heart were opened to the needs of prisoners. In that one visit to a prison, he saw–actually saw with his heart like the Samaritan–that prisoners are people who need and deserve God's grace as much as anyone.

When asked whether prisoners are "people in need," Steve answers with an array of statistics: 95 percent of prisoners will be released from prison one day; they have a 65–70 percent recidivism rate (in Tennessee) in the first eighteen months; it costs $50,000/year to keep someone in prison. His point is the economics of imprisonment should be enough to show us the value of helping prisoners get a fresh start on life. Beyond that, believers should be inspired to do this ministry through the words of the apostle Paul in his letter to Philemon, in which he encourages Philemon to receive Onesimus back as a member of the family and, therefore, treat him as such. Steve points out that many of us, especially respectable church folk, have the attitude of the elder brother in Jesus' parable of the Prodigal Son. Yet, if we can see prisoners as people whose needs merit our attention, we will do what we can to provide transitional housing, job training, employment counseling, and spiritual growth.

Steve Humphreys began his ministry by teaching *Experiencing God* one day a week in a prison in a neighboring county. As he watched prisoners' lives changed, he realized there was a ministry to this neglected people group. "Most of the people who go to prisons to try to reach the prisoners preach hell fire and damnation, but they don't reach many people. The men who go to the chapel services are already Christians. We reach men who don't go to chapel services and it's a lot more effective," Humphreys says.

Today he ministers to prisoners in four state prisons, three county jails, and a youth detention facility. In 2006 FOCUS had about 120 volunteers contribute more than two thousand hours of service, ministering to more than one thousand inmates, earning the ministry the honor of being named the Tennessee Department of Corrections' top East Tennessee Volunteer organization for 2007. FOCUS offers evangelism and discipleship classes, support groups, as well as "life preparation" classes in what he calls "Behind the Walls" settings. Additionally, the ministry provides help to men transitioning back into society in its "Beyond the Walls" ministry. As of this writing, FOCUS has aided about fifty men in making successful transitions into society. It maintains four "honor houses" where recently released or paroled prisoners may stay for little or no rent while they obtain employment and make other arrangements for productive living.

Not Just Them

A story that circulated several years ago, mostly in churches, talks about a reporter from the American media covering the violence in one of the Slavic countries. As the story goes, the reporter was watching an actual firefight among warring parties when a child innocently walking across the street was struck by a bullet. A man who lived in that town ran out into the street, gathered up the child and implored the reporter to take them to the nearest hospital in his car. Of course, the reporter agreed, loaded the man and wounded child into his car and set off for the hospital at breakneck speeds. As they rode through the city, the man in the back seat kept saying, "Please hurry, my child is dying!" In a matter of minutes, they arrived at the emergency room of the hospital, and the man ran inside with the child. He said to the medical staff, "My child has been shot! Please save her!" The reporter parked his car and went inside to see how the little girl was doing. He found the man pacing back and forth, wringing his hands in anxiety and fear. In a few minutes a nurse came out of the examining room and told the man the child had died despite their efforts to save her. "Oh, no!" he exclaimed. "What am I going to tell her father?!"

To this the reporter said, "I thought you said she was *your* child! You said 'Please hurry, my child is dying!'" The compassionate man looked at him and said, "They're *all* our children."

Now this may have happened, or it may only be a story—that is not the point. It still speaks a very important truth to us. This is the attitude that leads to lifestyle compassion ministry—to cease to see people in need as "them," people with whom we have no relationship and feel no responsibility. To see people in need, whether homeless, victims of poverty or disease or prisoners, as persons loved by God and targeted by God for special disbursements of his grace and mercy is to say, "It's not about us; it's about them." To see people in need as people who are not very different from us but people whose life circumstances have victimized them and placed them at the mercy of the rest of us who are more fortunate (not wiser or better) than they is to say, "It's not about us; it's about them." When that thought becomes part of our spiritual DNA, we are on our way to authentic lifestyle compassion ministry. And the world will be different because of it.

I have come to believe that a lot that goes on in the church today saddens the Father because, after all, it's not about us; it's about them.

- When we spend most of our resources and energy on ourselves, it makes God sad because...it's not about us; it's about them.

- When we talk and talk and talk about how we need to reach people in need and minister to them in Jesus' name but we never get beyond talk, it makes God sad because... it's not about us; it's about them.
- When we can't find a place in our crowded church calendars for one day to mobilize our people to get beyond the walls of the church to minister to "the least of these," it breaks God's heart because...it's not about us; it's about them.
- When we waste energy and spiritual vitality on petty issues that have absolutely nothing to do with the Kingdom—what color the carpet in the new building should be; whether we should wear a coat and tie to church or go casual; whether the pastor speaks to me today—it breaks God's heart because...it's not about us; it's about them.
- When we allow pride and "turfism" to prevent us from joining with other Christ-followers of other denominations and ethnic groups to reach our city for Christ, it breaks the Father's heart because...it's not about us; it's about them.
- When people in our communities who are far away from God do not see the church as a place where they can encounter the God of Abraham, Isaac, and Jacob, it breaks the Father's heart because...it's not about us; it's about them.
- When crime, poverty, and homelessness are running out of control in places where there is a church on every corner, it breaks the Father's heart because...it's not about us; it's about them.
- When the church becomes a club for members only and stained-glass windows are actually meant to separate and insulate insiders from outsiders, it breaks God's heart because...it's not about us; it's about them.
- When the nation is divided by race and socioeconomic standing and politics and the church does little or nothing to bring people together, it breaks God's heart because... it's not about us; it's about them.

At Thanksgiving, a young woman decided that rather than travel the three thousand miles to her family's home, she would volunteer at a local soup kitchen. She had never worked in a soup kitchen before and she had never even met a homeless person before. As Thanksgiving approached, she turned down several invitations to dinner, announcing—with a certain smugness—her plans for the day.

But when she arrived on Thanksgiving morning, dressed in jeans and T-shirt, the director of the soup kitchen announced that, for the first time ever, they had more than twice the volunteers they needed. He thanked everyone for coming, and added as a joke, "Of course, you're all invited to stay for lunch." Everyone laughed and quickly left for their own Thanksgiving dinners—everyone except for this young woman who had nowhere to go at that late notice. She stayed, got in line, and picked up a tray.

"Here you go, honey," said the woman serving turkey. "But I'm a volunteer. I'm not..." she said, but the woman was already serving the next person.

She found an empty place at a table. A man extended his dirty hand. "Hi, I'm Fred," he said. "I'm an alcoholic," he added, and went on to tell how he was on the road back. "That's nice," she said. "I was supposed to volunteer here..." "Oh," Fred said. His face fell and he turned to the man next to him.

A pregnant woman struggling to manage a toddler and two plates of food slid into a chair. "It's good to sit down," the woman smiled. "You know how it is—this is the first time I've been able to eat in peace for days!"

"I'll feed your son," the supposed-to-be volunteer offered. "Oh, would you? That's so kind." "Well, actually, I'm a volunteer. It's kind of my job..." "Oh." The woman's face clouded, and she ate quietly, not saying anything else.

A father and his son then took places next to her. "Daddy! Mmmmm! I like this food!" the boy said. "Don't eat too fast, son." The father turned to her and explained his son's exuberance: "It's been a while since I could afford to give him a good meal like this one. You know?"

"I'm a volunteer," she said quickly. The father's face turned red and there was awkwardness in the air.

"We got a volunteer in our class at school," the boy chimed in. "She sits right down at our table with us in school. You know, she teaches us better than our teacher—'cause she's right at the same table, not way up in the front of the room."

She looked at the happy little boy jabbing his plastic fork into the sweet potatoes. He had unwittingly put his finger right on the heart of the matter. She had been so busy looking for differences between her and everyone else that she was acting as if they were a separate species. But were they so different? Hadn't she had job and relationships problems? Didn't she have friends who were recovering alcoholics? And what about her own young niece who was already the mother of a toddler and an infant? What made these people less worthy of her care and love for them? She, the self-righteous volunteer, was really the guest–the welcomed guest–at *their* table.[20]

Notes

[1]Randy White, *Encounter God in the City* (Downers Grove, Ill.: InterVarsity Press, 2006), 51.

[2]Sharon Cohen, "A Day in the Life of the Homeless in America," posted on www.truthout.com, February 27, 2005.

[3]Posted on www.endhomelessness.org, January 10, 2007.

[4]Cohen, "A Day in the Life of the Homeless in America."

[5]Ibid.

[6]Ibid.

[7]From www.wikipedia.com.

[8]From "Who Are America's Poor Children: The Official Story," posted on www.nccp.org, December, 2006.

[9]Ibid.

[10]Timothy J. Keller, *Ministries of Mercy* (Phillipsburg, N.J.: P & R Publishing, 1997), 19.

[11]Philip Coltoff, quoted in Stephanie Armour, "What Recovery? Working Poor Struggle To Pay Bills," *USA Today*, posted June 9, 2004 at www.usatoday.com/money/economy/2004-06-08-low-wage-working-poor_x.htm.

[12]Ibid.

[13]In training churches to do Operation Inasmuch, I emphasize that the recipients of their help should not be members of their church, that they should focus their efforts beyond the membership of their congregation, but there are exceptions. When congregations successfully help their members take up a lifestyle of compassion ministry, there will be enough help for folk outside and inside the church.

[14]Paul Harris, "37 Million Poor Hidden in the Land of Plenty," *Tulsa Observer*, February 19, 2006.

[15]Armour, "What Recovery?"

[16]David Callahan, "Still with Us: Elderly Poverty in America," available at http://www.cheatingculture.com/stillwithus.htm.

[17]Ibid.

[18]Craig's List, Staten Island, July 15, 2007.

[19]Deitrich B., posted on the Prison Fellowship Web site, www.prisonfellowship.org.

[20]*Connections* (November 2004): 4.

5

We Need the Poor

In the Old Testament, the subject of the poor is the second most prominent theme. Idolatry is the first, and the two are often connected. In the New Testament, one out of every sixteen verses is about the poor!

JIM WALLIS

Don't let the title of this chapter turn you off, at least not before you read it and learn what it means. It may not be what you think.

How many times have you heard a person talk about his or her experience in helping people in need in terms of the benefits he or she received from it? Probably, it was something like this: "I went there to help them and *I* was the one who received the greatest blessing from what I did!" Some have called this the boomerang effect of compassion ministry—helping others comes back to us in the form of spiritual and emotional benefits. We go with the intent of helping others and are surprised at what the helping *does for us.*

I understand this to be a basic spiritual principle—namely, that giving gives back. The New Testament puts it this way: "It is more blessed to give than to receive" (Acts 20:35). This principle is not only applicable to the giving of money but also of time and compassion ministry. I would go so far as to say that this principle *especially* applies to compassion ministry, that the giving of self *always* results in blessing—whether or not it is anticipated, whether or not the recipient of the ministry ever expresses gratitude for it. The blessing or benefit is inherent in the rendering of ministry. It is a law of life as God made it. My experience is that this law is every bit as reliable and universal as physical laws that rule the planet, such as gravity, necessity of water for survival, and so forth.

Let me be clear about this. When you give yourself in compassion ministry—that is, when you do what you can either planned or spontaneously (as in the case of the Samaritan in Luke 10)—you will be blessed by it. I don't fully understand how this works. I just believe that authentic ministry always results in a blessing/benefit to the one who ministers.

Having said this, I need to add a clarifying word. Sometimes the boomerang effect has too much influence on how we encourage believers to get involved in compassion ministry. We appeal to their sense of self-satisfaction: "Do it because it will bless you! It will make you feel good!" Having been in the role of encouraging, inviting, and challenging church folk to do what they already know to do but do not do, I understand the temptation to appeal to that part of persons' values, and, if the truth be known, I have done my share of it. We know this approach works. It gets results. However, it encourages those we are inviting to get involved in compassion ministry to do so from lower motives, and, therefore, not to grow past them. Is it a better motive to serve at a homeless shelter because of how it will make me feel or because Jesus said we are to serve the poor? It is better to deliver groceries to persons each month who have limited resources because they are HIV positive because I know how good I will feel about it when I'm finished or because they need food and their money runs out before the end of each month?

It is true that it is better to give than to receive, but it is also true that we receive every time we give. But we do not give *in order to receive* but because we have something to give and because someone else needs it. Congregational leaders, especially pastors, understand the dynamic tension of this issue—wanting to see believers step outside their comfort zone to minister to people they do not know, but also wanting them to do the right thing *for the right reason.* Jesus was all about motives. His harshest criticism was reserved for those who did the right things but for the wrong reasons. So, we must appeal to persons' sense of obedience and compassion for the poor, not to their desire to "get a blessing."

Now, let's return to the concept of "we need the poor." This phrase refers to the fact that we *need* to serve others. Serving others, especially people for whom we have no stated responsibility, is a basic need on the level of food, water, and shelter. I believe this is true for all people whether or not they are followers of Jesus, but it is especially true of Christ-followers. It is the nature of God's love to give to others, particularly to "the least of these," or those whose needs are conspicuous or arresting. John goes so far as to say that serving people in need is the test of whether or not God's love is in us.

> If anyone says, "I love God," yet hates his brother, he is a liar. For anyone who does not love his brother, whom he has seen, cannot love God, whom he has not seen. And he has given us this command: Whoever loves God must also love his brother. (1 Jn. 4:20–21)

I have tried to make the best case I know how for the idea that compassion ministry is an important aspect of discipleship. In this chapter I take that idea to another level. I believe it is *necessary*. Compassion ministry is a necessary part of what it means to follow Jesus because that is what he did, and following Jesus means to do what he did. But it is also necessary because God's love in us needs an outlet. So, *we need* people in need because they are the best "outlet" or recipients of Jesus' love through us, his ministers. As a coach needs a team to lead and a teacher needs at least one student, so believers need people in need to serve in order to be authentic followers of Jesus.

A friend said it this way. A chair has four legs to hold us up. When we sit in a chair with a missing leg, we fall. The chair needs all four legs. Compassion is a basic component of the Christian life.

A few years ago, Michael Elliot published a provocative book entitled *Playing Hide & Seek,* in which he gives some off-the-wall ideas of where God is and what God cares about. I say "off-the-wall," not because I think he is wrong in what he says, but because his ideas are most definitely unconventional. He includes in the book the following "Reasons Why God Wants Us to Play with Poor People":

- God wants to remind all of us that we are God's children and are to act like one big happy family that should have more to do with one another.
- Like most parents, God gives the most attention to the children experiencing the most problems while asking the other brothers and sisters to help out.
- Like most children, when God focuses extra attention on a brother or sister, we act up, often by throwing a spiritual temper tantrum, in an attempt to get the spotlight back on us.
- God wants to remind us that no matter how much help we need, someone else always needs more.
- God wants to remind us that no matter how little we have, someone else always has less, so we should be thankful for what we have.
- God wants to remind us that we all have the ability to make a significant difference in someone else's life.
- God wants us to know that being involved with the poor makes us quit thinking so much about ourselves–and God wants us to think less about ourselves.
- God wants us to think about new things, and poor people force us to think about things we would usually never consider.
- God wants us to try new things, and poor people force us to do things we would usually never consider.
- Being involved with poor people forces us to rely on God when looking for a solution to problems too overwhelming to solve on our own.[1]

Serving Jesus

Jesus spoke about serving people in need in the most appealing terms. He said when we minister to them, we are ministering to him (Mt. 25). Jesus was not speaking figuratively, nor was he just trying to motivate us to serve "the least of these." To assume that is *nonsense!* I think he meant exactly what he said. The Jesus who calmed a violent storm with his voice and healed a woman who merely touched the hem of his clothes is capable of being spiritually present in the persons of need we encounter on the highways of life. The Jesus who was raised from the dead is capable of being wherever he chooses, whenever he chooses, and in whomever he chooses—including the poor, the oppressed, and the hopeless. Jesus has been freed from the limits of time and space. And, if we know anything at all about his priorities, about the people with whom he felt most comfortable, about his feeling for the poor and marginalized, then why should it be inconceivable that he does not dwell with them?

Who would not do anything and everything possible to minister to Jesus if he were suddenly to appear on our doorstep? The question is whether we see him when he appears. An excerpt from my first book will explain:

> We can miss him if we are not alert. After all, he will not appear to us with a halo over his head looking like the picture in your grandmother's house—soft, brown eyes, long, black hair, and a full beard. He is not about to walk up to us and say, "Shalom. I'm Jesus of Nazareth. Want to see a miracle?" He's not that obvious and noticeable, but he *is* here.
>
> He is the abused wife who dreads to hear her alcoholic husband come home at night because she doesn't know whether she will get through the night without a beating. He is the misfit teenager who does not know how it feels to be accepted by his peers, who would rather take a beating than go to school where he is ridiculed and persecuted unmercifully. He is the wealthy woman who has always had anything she wants in the way of material things but yearns for the one thing she does not have—real friends who accept her for herself, not because of her money. He is the pregnant teenager who is scared and lonely and confused, who wants to do the right thing about her baby but wonders if she can, if she can provide a decent home for the child when it is born and wonders if she has just sealed her fate for the rest of her life. He is the homeless man pushing a shopping cart with all his worldly

possessions, sleeping in the woods, under overpasses, and in cardboard boxes, taking meals at the Salvation Army or wherever he can find them. Jesus is, dare I say it, the AIDS patient who is cut off from everyone because they are afraid of him, who is dying with hardly anyone to comfort him.

If I understand Matthew 25, Jesus is most definitely all of these persons and a multitude of other hurting people. But we seldom recognize him. He is here, but we do not see him.[2]

If we believe this and if we take Matthew 25 at face value, then we *need* the poor because they provide opportunities for us to serve Jesus. They give us opportunities to show our love for him. Authentic love expresses itself. It cannot remain silent or it is not real love. Any married man knows how to demonstrate his love for his wife. It may be flowers with no special occasion, or even a *particular* kind of flower (my wife loves daisies). It may be an unplanned weekend excursion away from children and home responsibilities. It may be a poem or spontaneous and warm note of love. And when he wants to let his wife know how much he loves her, he shows her in her preferred way.

In Matthew 25, Jesus is letting us know how he prefers to be loved. If we love him, we will show him. That's a given. The only question is how. Jesus' preferred way for us to show him that we love him is to minister to people in need. So, we need the poor! Phil Kenneson, professor of theology at Milligan College, says it well in his book *Cultivating a Generous Heart:*

> The notion that we might not simply take Jesus to the poor, but just as importantly, meet Jesus *in* the poor, might run counter to our normal ways of thinking... But it's quite possible that in reaching out to the poor and oppressed of our neighborhoods and the world, we too will be converted. Converted from our own prejudiced opinions of those who are different from us. Converted from our own constricted views of God's work in the world. Converted from our own narrow understanding of the gospel of Jesus Christ.[3]

Aware of Human Need

As I am writing this portion of this chapter, I am in New Orleans attending a convention in which the book on Operation Inasmuch was taught as a missions study. I was invited to address the closing session of the convention to encourage them to follow through with implementation of what they just learned about community ministry. It has been one of the most affirming and encouraging experiences of my short tenure as the leader of Operation Inasmuch, Inc.

My travel plans left me in New Orleans for an additional day following the close of the convention, so I took a Grey Line Tour of the city to see the damages caused by Hurricane Katrina. Our guide explained what happened to several areas of the city and the damages that resulted from the unbelievable flooding in the wake of Katrina. We saw water marks high up on buildings, markings still visible from the inspection of homes as soon as rescue personnel could get to them, and repaired levies. Our convention met in the New Orleans Convention Center–where television cameras and reporters had again and again shown the awful chaos of the aftermath of the hurricane and flood.

Like you, I saw what the media showed us for weeks following Katrina. I prayed for the victims and their families. I sent money. And like many of you, I made a couple of trips to the Gulf region to help repair some of the homes destroyed by the hurricane. Even so, it was important for me to see what happened to this community, to see how their lives were devastated, and to learn about their pain, which is far from resolved even now, two years later. I needed to see it myself in order to understand.

This is the point I am making about needing the poor. They remind us of the harsher realities of life. They help us remember that life is not comfortable or even safe for everyone. They expose us to the ravages of poverty and oppression and ignorance. We need the poor to keep us informed about their need. It is still true, isn't it: out of sight, out of mind? When people in need are out of sight, and they are for most of us, they are out of mind.

We are all creatures of habit. We move about in the same traffic patterns almost all of the time. Most of us rarely go into the pockets of despair that exist in our communities. We don't see them because we don't go there. Consequently, we forget that some children go to bed hungry. We forget that there are people who do not have jobs or homes. We forget that there are millions of people who are victimized by greed and injustice. We forget that young girls get pregnant out of ignorance and bring into the world children who have almost no chance of breaking out of the cycle of poverty that has held every generation of their family as long as anyone can remember. We forget that elderly people often have to choose between buying food and buying their meds. We forget that some people wake up every morning and go to bed every night wondering how on earth they are going to make it through another day. We forget because we don't see.

This is why we need the poor. We need them to remind us that they exist. We need them to show us what life is like for people less fortunate than us. Without them—that is, without seeing them—we might forget. No, we *will* forget. And the consequences of that forgetting are catastrophic. We keep all we have to ourselves. We allow ourselves to believe all is well…everywhere. We never venture out of our comfort zone to interact with, much less *serve*, people in need. Perhaps the most surprising consequence of the out-of-sight-out-of-mind reality is that we—the haves—live impoverished lives. Not impoverished in the same way that the poor live, but impoverished from the truth about our world. And, as many daily newspapers in their masthead remind us: what we don't know *does* hurt us.

In New Orleans, our guide reminded us again and again that the city still has a long way to go in recovering from the worst natural (and bureaucratic) disaster in U.S. history. Even two full years after Katrina and its aftermath, there are plenty of signs that full recovery is years away. Our guide openly acknowledged the progress that has been made and the many people from all over the country who have contributed money and sweat to make this progress possible, but he wanted us to remember that more is needed. He wasn't asking for money but simply that we not forget the brave people of New Orleans who are struggling to finish the job. He said the same thing about his city I am trying to say about people in need the world over: we need them to remind us that they exist and their needs have not gone away. Just because the sun comes out after a storm, even a devastating hurricane, it doesn't mean that all is well again.

Purpose for Life

Why are you here? Why were you born? What is your purpose in life? If you cannot answer these questions, then you live
with some sense of emptiness. Even if you have learned how to
silence your deepest yearnings for purpose and meaning, you
know they are there, and every once in a while they resurface to
haunt you.

A few years ago, Rick Warren, senior pastor of the Saddleback
Community Church in California, had the whole country asking
these questions in his book *The Purpose Driven Life* (Zondervan,
2002). His summary question was: What on earth are you here
for? The Purpose Driven materials have guided thousands of
congregations and tens of thousands of believers through a process
of rediscovery of God's purposes for all people. The point was to
awaken in believers everywhere a sense of purpose for life, the
kind of purpose that would lead us into meaningful experiences
that make a difference not only for us but also for others, the kind
of purpose that brings deep satisfaction and peace. I have no way
of knowing how successful he was in accomplishing his goals, but
I applaud Warren and the Saddleback Church for raising such
important questions. They are questions we should face regularly
to ensure that we are fulfilling our purpose for being here. No
doubt such reflection plays a large part in Rick and Kay Warren's
passionate involvement in their three foundations, which are
helping people worldwide.

All of this is to say that the poor help us find meaning in life.
Serving them with authentic compassion gives meaning. It would
be easy to slip into another discourse similar to the one at the
beginning of this chapter, in which I remind you of the benefit or
blessing that comes with serving others, but I will do my best to
avoid that pitfall. What I am thinking of here is that serving the
poor gives meaning in that it is behavior that matters. It matters
whether people have enough food to eat, and when we help to feed
them, we know we are making a difference for them. It matters
whether children feel loved and have the necessities by which to
live, and when we show that we love them by teaching them how
to read better or providing a bed in which they can sleep each
night, it makes a difference. It matters whether pregnant teenage
girls who have been told by their families to leave have a safe

place to live and a few things by which to begin caring for their yet unborn children. It matters when we demonstrate our caring by giving them baby showers and fixing up the home for unwed mothers in which they are living. It makes a difference. These expressions of Christian compassion make a difference for those helped *and for us.*

Consider the story of Lynne McCauley. Several years ago she was unchurched and far away from God. She was invited by friends to help out at a block party sponsored by the friends' church. She and her family went along and were surprised that they enjoyed themselves. When they were invited to attend church with their friends, they went and Lynne found God there. Here is the rest of her story as reported in an article on the Leadership Network Web site (www.leadnet.org).

> Preparing to turn 40, Lynne announced to her family and friends, "I'm going back to Italy for my birthday, and it's going to be all about me!" Interestingly, details about a mission trip to Brazil started to appear in the church bulletin around the same time. One morning in prayer, Lynne realized that if she truly wanted her 40th year to be meaningful, it needed to be about service to others, not service to herself. Lynne's "all about me" birthday trip changed to an "all about God" trip to Brazil.
>
> In Brazil, Lynne says, "God broke my heart over the people of Brazil." She found herself grieving over what grieves God. "I was a wreck—the wheels completely came off my wagon." One of the first questions she asked her husband when she got off the plane was, "Can we sell our house and move to Brazil and start a mission training center? I struggled to reconcile the poverty I had seen there with the affluence in our community. I struggled with our lifestyle and materialism."

She began attending a local inner-city outreach program on the weekends. Lynne shares about her life-changing community service experience:

> "I sat down to have breakfast with two homeless men and talk about life on the streets. As we were talking, one of the men began to have a seizure. I was a critical care

nurse for 11 years so I was familiar with the scenario and helped lay him on the ground and to talk to him during the episode. As I knelt beside him on the floor and talked, he kept his vision locked on me, and I on him. The paramedics arrived and began to minister to him in a cold and impersonal way. All the while he kept locked on me. As they bundled him on the gurney and prepared to roll him out to the ambulance, he pulled down his oxygen mask, looked me directly in the eye and whispered, 'Thank you.' I looked at his man–dirty, unkempt, vomit on his beard and smelling of alcohol and urine–and I thought to myself, 'I am looking into the face of Christ.' I knew right then that I was right where God wanted me and I have been involved ever since."

Lynne is currently serving as the director of externally focused initiatives at her church in Carmel, Indiana. She says: "I have never been happier in my life. I didn't set out to work in ministry, but in my search to find more meaning in my life, I discovered my promised land."[4]

One of the most basic needs of all people is a sense of worth. All people need to know their lives matter–that they are not just taking up space on the planet, but rather are making a difference somehow, some way. Study after study verifies our need of worth. Serving others, especially those whose needs are compelling, fulfills our need for self-worth. Nothing so satisfies our need for self-worth as doing for others. How else can we explain the fact that young people continue to be trained to be schoolteachers? They surely know teachers do not make much money compared to other professions. They probably know how very challenging it is to overcome the many obstacles to learning created by an unruly, hostile school environment and uncooperative parents to accomplish the learning they desire in their students. But they continue to sign up, and thank goodness they do. Part of the reason is that these young people know that teaching is one way to make a lasting difference for children and for the communities where they live. They are driven by their desire to serve–not to make money or to become powerful or even to be admired, but to serve through teaching. Serving through teaching gives them meaning, and, hopefully, this vision is reinforced sufficiently by former students who let them know what a difference their teachers made for them.

When I was in the sixth grade, I was a poor student–lazy, unmotivated, and unproductive. My teacher encouraged me again and again by telling me I could do better if I would just put forth a little effort. She saw potential in me I did not see. She recorded her encouragement on my report cards for my parents to see, but I never got the message. I went throughout that year making just average grades with little or no effort. It was not until my second year in college that my academic abilities awakened. I went on to earn graduate degrees, including a doctorate, with high marks. I never forgot Mrs. Brantley, my sixth grade teacher. A few years ago, I was invited back to the church where she is a member to preach a series of renewal messages. In one of those messages, I looked at Mrs. Brantley, long since retired from teaching, and reminded her of what she told me many years earlier. I told her I never forgot what she said and eventually acted on it. Her investment in me was not lost even though it surely looked that way at the end of my sixth grade experience. I did that because I wanted Mrs. Brantley to know she made a difference for me. Her confidence in me mattered. And I trust that my comments to her added to the meaning of her life.

Serving the poor also gives purpose in life by building up the community. Another of our basic needs is community. God made us communal beings. We need each other. Any time we can strengthen the community, we enhance our own sense of security and well-being, and serving the poor strengthens the community. And when we can chip away at the pockets of despair in all of our communities by giving hope to some who have lost it, the entire community benefits and we know we have made a difference.

When I train churches to use the Operation Inasmuch model of community ministry, I tell them it provides a way to transform their community. I am honest in making this assertion. I do not encourage them to think that just one Operation Inasmuch will make all that is harmful in their community go away, but rather that ongoing compassion ministry in the areas of their community where despair runs high will actually change the way people live their lives. I tell them of something that happened several years ago in a small town in eastern North Carolina. A white congregation had a good experience with Operation Inasmuch and invited a black congregation to join them in this community ministry. Each time, the two congregations came together to celebrate what God did for their community through them.

In one of these celebrations, a member of the black church stood and said, "You white folks may not have noticed that the color of my skin is lighter than that of my brothers and sisters in my church, but they notice and they know why." She went on to tell of a rape of one of her ancestors a couple of generations earlier by a white man, resulting in a mixed-blood birth of which she was a descendent. Then she said, "It has taken me putting on work gloves and blue jeans and getting down on my hands and knees to do landscaping work with you folks from [the white church] to begin to let go of some of the bitterness I have felt for years." Some time later, a descendent of the white man responsible for the rape years earlier—and a member of that white congregation—died. His family invited this woman and her family to sit with his family at the funeral, which took place in the white church.

That's community transformation, and it was brought about through compassion ministry. It would be hard to see how anyone who participated in that ministry did not have a stronger sense of purpose after that experience. Because those two congregations came together to minister to people in need in their community, God brought about transformation that might not have come any other way. And that experience in turn enhanced the sense of purpose for those who were part of the experience. The people in need in that community contributed to this transformation by simply being there and receiving the ministry offered them.

Spiritual Growth

Another way people in need help us is that they provide significant opportunities for spiritual growth. When I train congregational leaders to conduct an Operation Inasmuch in their church and community, I tell them that one of the benefits of using this model is that it fortifies believers' faith. Whenever we do something we say we believe, then our belief is made stronger. In other words, when we give a day to minister to people in need, our belief in ministering to people in need becomes stronger, and when we discuss that belief with friends and family, the strength of our conviction will come through, probably illustrated by our most recent experience of compassion ministry.

More to the point, it has been reported to me on numerous occasions that compassion ministry strengthens persons' discipleship. It makes better believers. It contributes to their spiritual growth as do prayer, worship, giving, and other spiritual disciplines. Actually, it has been found that compassion ministry does more to stimulate spiritual growth than these other, traditional spiritual behaviors.

However, we do far less to encourage believers to give themselves in some expression of compassion ministry than any of the other spiritual disciplines we can name. We set aside special times for prayer and call it prayer meeting. We conduct stewardship campaigns, in some cases annually, partly because giving is essential to continued church life. We provide for and urge our folk to participate fully in worship because worship is part of what it means to be followers of Jesus. But we are not as faithful about helping our fellow believers find appropriate places to serve people in need, even though we would universally agree that serving them is basic to the Christian life. But if we remember the value of compassion ministry to spiritual growth, and if we listen to the voice inside us that is telling us there has to be more to the Christian life than mere participation in church activities, there is a chance we will see compassion ministry as one of the ways we can improve our "followship" of Jesus.

A study conducted by the School of Social Work at Baylor University in 2006 confirms the value of community service for spiritual growth. The study investigated the impact of community service on churchgoing teenagers and found that it has an undeniable influence on their spiritual development. The study examined the experiences of 631 teens in thirty-five congregations of various denominations spread across six states. The researchers found that "teenagers who were involved in community ministry through their congregations scored significantly higher on the Faith Maturity Scale [a spiritual assessment instrument] and on the degree to which they practice their faith in daily life."[5] When the researchers analyzed the data carefully their conclusion was as follows: "These findings suggest that those who want to help young people develop a rigorous, meaningful faith life should involve them in meaningful service."[6]

Therefore, I do not think it goes too far to say that people in need help us grow spiritually. Though I do not have empirical data to support it, I suspect that the spiritual growth that comes through giving ourselves in authentic compassion ministry to people in need is unique. To put it another way, we *cannot* be all Jesus called us to be without the poor.

Beggars Looking for Beggars

The following story seals my attempt to make a case for the importance of people in need for those of us who would take up lifestyle compassion ministry. It comes from Dr. Paul Brand in his book *Fearfully and Wonderfully Made*.

> The concept of service is best communicated through a personal example rather than through an abstract discussion, and a powerful memory edges into my mind of a strange-looking Frenchman named Abbé Pierre. He arrived at the leprosy hospital at Vellore [which Dr. Brand founded and ran in India] wearing his simple monk's habit and carrying a blanket over his shoulders and one carpetbag containing everything he possessed. I invited him to stay at my home, and there he told me his story.
>
> As a Catholic friar he had been assigned to work among the beggars in Paris after World War II. At that time beggars in that city had nowhere to go, and in winter many of them would freeze to death in the streets. Abbé Pierre began by trying to interest the community in the beggars' plight, but was unsuccessful. He decided the only recourse was to show the beggars how to mobilize themselves. First, he taught them to do their tasks better. Instead of sporadically collecting bottles and rags, they organized into teams to scour the city. Next, he led them to build a warehouse from discarded bricks and start a business in which they sorted vast amounts of used bottles from big hotels and businesses. Finally Pierre inspired each beggar by giving him responsibility to help another beggar poorer than himself. Then the project really began to succeed. An

organization called Emmaus was founded to perpetuate Pierre's work, with branches in other countries.

Now, he told me, after years of this work in Paris, there were no beggars left in that French city. Pierre believed his organization was about to face a serious crisis.

"I must find somebody for my beggars to help!" he declared and had begun searching in other places around the world. It was during one of those trips that he had come to Vellore. He concluded by describing his dilemma. "If I don't find people worse off than my beggars, this movement could turn inward. They'll become a powerful, rich organization and the whole spiritual impact will be lost! They'll have no one to serve." As we walked out of the house toward the student hostel to have lunch, my head was ringing with Abbé Pierre's earnest for "somebody for my beggars to help!"[7]

This is precisely the attitude I want to inspire in all my readers. I want you to see the value the poor have for you. They can do for you what no one else can. They can renew your sense of purpose in life, or give you one to begin with. They make it possible for you to serve Jesus in the way he prefers. And they provide an outlet for God's love in you that cries out for expression. If their need is not enough to cause you to take up a lifestyle of compassion ministry, then let them be used by God to bring you where God wants you to be—far away from the holy huddle you call church and into the community where God is.

As captivating as Dr. Brand's story is above, it has an even better ending, and while it may not illustrate directly my point in this chapter, it is far too good not to tell the rest of it.

We had a tradition among the medical students at Vellore about which I warned all guests in advance. All lunchtime guests would stand and say a few words about who they were and why they had come. Like students everywhere, ours were lighthearted and ornery, and they had developed an unspoken three-minute tolerance rule. If any guest talked longer than three minutes (or became boring before that time was up), the students would stamp their feet and make the person sit down.

On the day of Pierre's visit, he stood up and I introduced him to the group. I could see the Indian students eyeing him quizzically–this small man with a big nose and nothing attractive about him, wearing a peculiar old habit. Pierre was speaking in French, and a fellow worker named Heinz and I strained to translate what he was saying. Neither of us was well-practiced in French, since no one in that part of India spoke it, so we could only break in here and there with a summary sentence.

Abbé Pierre began slowly but soon speeded up, like a tape recorder turning too fast, with sentences spilling over each other, gesticulating all the while. I was extremely tense because he was going into the whole history of the movement, and I knew the students would soon shout down this great, humble man. Worse, I was failing miserably to translate his rapid-fire sentences…Pierre was saying that you don't need language to express love, only to express hate. The language of love is what you *do*. Then he spoke faster and faster, and Heinz and I looked at each other and shrugged helplessly.

Three minutes passed, and I stepped back and looked around the room. No one moved. The Indian students gazed at Pierre with piercing black eyes, their faces rapt. He went on and on, and no one interrupted. After twenty minutes Pierre sat down, and immediately the students burst into the most tremendous ovation I ever heard in that hall.

Completely mystified, I had to question some of the students. "How did you understand? No one here speaks French."

One student answered me, "We did not need a language. We felt the presence of God and the presence of love."

Abbé Pierre had learned the discipline of loyal service… He had come to India and found leprosy patients to fulfill his desperate search to find someone worse off than his beggars, and when he found them, he was filled with love and joy. He returned to France, and they and Emmaus worked to donate a ward at the hospital in Vellore.[8]

Notes

[1]Michael Elliot, *Playing Hide & Seek* (Macon, Ga.: Smyth and Helwys, 1996), 43–44.

[2]David Crocker, *Operation Inasmuch: Mobilizing Believers beyond the Walls of the Church* (St. Louis: Chalice Press, 2005), 65–66.

[3]Phillip D. Kenneson, *Cultivating a Generous Heart* (Cincinnati: Standard Publishing, 2005), 260, available through www.christianstandard.com.

[4]Krista Petty, "Six Catalytic Service Approaches," article posted on the Leadership Network Web site, www.leadnet.org, 13–14.

[5]Michael E. Sherr, "The Role of Community Service in the Faith Development of Adolescents," unpublished study by the School of Social Work (Baylor University, 2006), 11.

[6]Ibid.

[7]Paul Brand and Philip Yancey, *Fearfully and Wonderfully Made* (Grand Rapids: Zondervan, 1980), 71–72.

[8]Ibid., 72–74.

6

Turn Your Chairs Around

There are those who seek knowledge for the sake of knowledge.
That is curiosity.
There are those who seek knowledge to be known by others.
That is vanity.
There are those who seek knowledge in order to serve.
That is love.

BERNARD OF CLAIRVAUX

It's easy for the needs or interests of insiders to ultimately drive
the priorities of any organization. It's just the natural tendency
of any group to become insider-focused. If you are surrounded
long enough by people who think like you think, you will become
more and more certain that's the best way to think.

ANDY STANLEY, REGGIE JOINER, LANE JONES

Powerful images tend to be simple yet poignant. The preacher
was telling his audience about his church's efforts to assimilate new
members into their congregation and, at the same time, mobilize
them back into the community in authentic ministry. He described
the various themes of new member classes, which he teaches
himself. In the last class he has the participants get up out of their
chairs (which are formed in a circle), face the chairs outward, and
sit down again. Then he says to them something like, "As long as

we are facing our circle inward, all we see is each other. But when we face our chairs outward, look how much bigger the world is and how many more people there are in that world. In this church we sit with our chairs facing outward." It cannot be a surprise that this pastor was invited to the Externally Focused Church Conference or that his church is one of the model congregations held up before those of us attending the conference as an example of how God is remaking the church.

I have attended my share of church conferences in three decades of ministry, almost all of them while in the pastorate. A few of them have moved me to make significant changes in my ministry, but most of them have merely served as a nice diversion from the everyday routines of ministry without having any impact on the way I do church. The Externally Focused Church Conference was different partly because, for the first time ever, I was in a room with hundreds of other ministry leaders who share my calling and commitment to compassion ministry, and partly because it confirmed what I had been feeling for some time—that God is remaking the church by facing her outward.

This sort of confirmation can have a powerful effect on us. It helps us see that our efforts have not been misdirected, that we have been right in our sense of leading from the Father and not merely following our own passions, and that we are part of something far bigger than ourselves. Such was my experience at the Externally Focused Church Conference. I felt I was with family. There were no more than three or four persons I knew there, yet I felt among family in that we shared a calling from God to lead people to lifestyle compassion ministry. In this chapter I want to reproduce this feeling for you. I realize that it is not possible to give you that same sense of being part of something bigger than yourself in a single chapter—or in an entire book, for that matter. Nevertheless, I want you to see what I am convinced is a fresh movement of God in the church, trusting God may use it to encourage and inspire you further toward lifestyle compassion ministry.

A New Reformation

In his salient and immensely popular book *The Present Future*, Reggie McNeal faces his readers with six new realities in church life. Reality number three is: "A New Reformation." His point is that much of what we see happening in churches today, such as the chaos of the worship wars, the disintegration of traditional structures, and a host of other issues, are the work of God remaking the church. He says what I have been saying privately and not nearly as well. This is nothing short of another reformation like the one that occurred in the sixteenth century in Europe and changed the Church forever.

> The first Reformation was about freeing the church. The new Reformation is about freeing God's people from the church (the institution). The original Reformation decentralized the church. The new Reformation decentralizes ministry. The former Reformation occurred when clergy were no longer willing to take marching orders for their ministry from the Pope. The current Reformation finds church members no longer willing for clergy to script their personal spiritual ministry journey. The last Reformation moved the church closer to home. The new Reformation is moving the church closer to the world. The historic Reformation distinguished Christians one from the other. The current Reformation is distinguishing followers of Jesus from religious people. The European Reformation assumed the church to be a part of the cultural-political order. The Reformation currently under way does not rely on the cultural-political order to prop up the church. The initial Reformation was about church. The new Reformation is about mission.[1]

McNeal makes a good point when he says that, similar to the first one, this new Reformation is fueled by an information revolution. Whereas the printing press made the Bible and Luther's writings available to the masses, the Internet and all of its auxiliary endeavors have placed an incredible amount of information at the fingertips of anyone willing to look at a computer screen. I had assumed it was God's dissatisfaction with the institutional church that was the reason for the upheaval we see in church life these days, and I still believe that is *a* reason, if not the ultimate one. After all, the record (the Bible) shows that there are limits to God's patience; God eventually starts over when his people are stubborn in their disobedience and self-centered ways. But

McNeal's point is well taken. The explosion of communication and access to information has forever changed our world, and church life is not exempt from these changes. "The result is that church members no longer have to rely on clergy for information about theology or Christian activity in the world. Nor do they have to rely on denominations to structure their giving or ministry focus. Increasingly, these are individual choices, driven by a sense of personal mission, not mere underwriting of the church or denominational program by faithful loyalists."[2]

My purpose here is not to analyze the fresh movement of God to face his church outward, but rather to announce it and celebrate it. As one writer puts it: "A powerful transformation is happening as churches across the nation are realizing a potent truth: God is at work extending his reign through acts of service to local communities. These acts of service are making a deep-rooted impact."[3]

It's a Big World

I suppose we all tend to think our small world–the realm of our knowledge, experience, and influence–is all God is doing in the world. But the true test of God's work includes whether we see signs of it elsewhere. It is a big world. God is a big God. How foolish is it to think that what he is doing with me is totally unique? How much more affirming is it when I see God is leading me where God is leading others at the same time?

Several years after we developed the model of community ministry that is Operation Inasmuch, I began to hear of other, similar models that are accomplishing the same thing in churches across the country. Honestly, I was a little disappointed at first. My pride and ambition had led me to think I was special, that I was on to something that was unique and, of course, would lead to the notoriety for which I yearned. But I soon realized that God was confirming my calling to lead congregations to immerse themselves in compassion ministry by showing me that he was raising up others who were doing the same thing. That is when I understood that community ministry is a movement of God.

Eric Swanson of the Externally Focused Network agrees wholeheartedly that God is definitely up to something. He cites the proliferation of externally focused ministries surfacing all over the world as one sign of this movement of God, but he also cites the fresh wave of interest in serving the poor and ending poverty in such high profile figures as Bill Gates, Warren Buffett, and Bono. He sees some similarity between these developments and Old Testament history when God used non-Hebrews to accomplish his agenda, people such as Cyrus and Artaxerxes. He recognizes some of the philanthropy making headlines these days as the work of God whether or not those responsible indicate they are led by God to do what they do. He understands that God may be saying to the traditional church: I'd love to use you, but you're investing in the wrong things, constructing huge buildings in which to gather your own rather than ministering to the poor.

Swanson sees the next wave of compassion ministry as congregations working not so much *for* the community but *with* the community. He anticipates the day when compassion ministry is a way of life for most churches and church folk and that it is done in what he calls "a non-dominating way." That is, that people come together around things and other people they care about in a God-rich environment that spawns other conversations. No one can tell where such things will lead.

I do not assume that you are aware of the many compassion ministry models available these days. While space does not allow me to catalogue all of them, I do want to introduce some of those I know to be effective, and which are utilized by a sufficient number of churches to verify their effectiveness. A brief description of these models follows.

Externally Focused Churches

Eric Swanson and Rick Rusaw wrote *The Externally Focused Church* in 2004. As much as any single volume, God has used it to inspire congregational leaders throughout the nation to tell their fellow believers to face their chairs outward. From that one book a number of significant contributions to the movement of God among his church have come. Simultaneous to the Externally Focused Church Conference I described at the beginning of this chapter was the launching of the Externally Focused Network. This will be a loose network of ministries and churches that share a commitment to see the church face outward and incarnate God's love for local communities. At an informal gathering of ministry leaders who led workshops at the conference, Rick Rusaw shared his conviction that all this is indeed a movement of God. Rusaw, Swanson and their colleagues in Leadership Network are establishing the Externally Focused Network to get in on what God is doing. You can learn more about this initiative at www.leadnet. org and click on the "Externally Focused Churches" page.

ShareFest (www.sharefest.org)

In 1998 a group of pastors in Central Arkansas came together in a Pastors' Prayer Summit. The result of that transforming experience was reconciliation and renewal of relationships among the pastors as well as a commitment to reach their community for Christ through compassion ministry. The following year they launched ShareFest, a combined effort by many churches to minister to the poor and marginalized in the Little Rock, Arkansas, area. Eight years later this endeavor is not only a respected part of the larger movement of God to face the church outward but also a movement in itself. The ShareFest Web site lists communities all over America where ShareFest events are held, regularly mobilizing thousands of believers beyond the walls of their churches in compassion ministry. The following statement from the site evinces God's use of ShareFest to advance his remaking of the church:

> It has truly become the catalyst that has helped many churches connect with their communities and to become more outwardly focused throughout the year. New relationships have been established between churches, schools, community leaders, and non-profit organizations. This simple idea of uniting together with other churches to demonstrate the love of Christ is now spreading to many *ShareFest Cities* all across the country.[4]

Kingdom Assignment (www.kingdomassignment.com)

In 2000, Denny Bellisi, pastor of Coastal Hills Community Church in California, challenged one hundred people in his congregation to receive $100 from the church's funds and "reinvest" it according to the parable of talents in Matthew and bring back to the church what God did with their investment in ninety days. Stories poured in over the next few months about everything from serving homeless persons to building a home for battered women. Now Kingdom Assignment is a national ministry empowering congregations across the country to use this method of mobilizing their people into community ministry.

Kingdom Assignment has been expanded to KA 2 and KA 3. KA 2 is a challenge for believers to sell a personal possession and give the proceeds to the poor or to an organization that ministers to the poor and, where possible, to become involved in that ministry. KA 3 involves a person giving of that person's time to an individual in need. "Participants are commissioned to give of themselves to one person they consider to be among 'the least of these' for 90 concentrated minutes of time and return in 90 days with an account of their experience."[5]

JustFaith (www.justfaith.org)

While serving as a priest in a Catholic parish in Louisville, Kentucky, Jack Jezreel developed a course of study combined with community ministry known as JustFaith. It is a program designed to empower and expand parish and church commitment to social ministry. On his Web site, Jezreel offers the following description of how his ministry began:

> Instead of preparing participants for initiation into the Catholic Church, I wanted to prepare participants to become prophets and dedicated servants of God's compassion. I devoted the curriculum to the Church's tradition of care for the vulnerable including the Scriptural evidence, historical witness and Catholic social teaching. I bundled these together, called the program JustFaith and offered the program for the first time in 1989, not knowing if anyone would be interested. To my delight, twelve people signed up that year. To my disbelief and endless gratitude, the results were staggering.[6]

In 2007, almost three hundred parishes and churches, with about three thousand people, are expected to participate in this rapidly growing ministry. If a movement is like the tide that rolls in, covering land that was previously uncovered and thereby changing the landscape, then JustFaith is one of the waves moving the ocean of God's grace where God wants it to be.

Operation Inasmuch (www.operationinasmuch.com)

The story of Operation Inasmuch is carefully documented in my book *Operation Inasmuch: Mobilizing Believers Beyond the Walls of the Church.*[7] It began as an attempt by Snyder Memorial Baptist Church in Fayetteville, North Carolina, simply to connect with our community in ways that responded to some of our neighbors' needs in one day of compassion ministry. At the time we had no intention of conducting this community ministry event more than once, but God had other plans. God led us to hone the event into a model of community ministry, then to document it and share it with anyone interested in knowing about it. Twelve years later, Operation Inasmuch is being done in ten states and two other countries (Canada and England) by several hundred churches. Earlier this year (2007), I responded to God's call for me to give the remainder of my life to the use of Operation Inasmuch in leading congregations worldwide to develop a culture of compassion ministry both in their church life and in their communities. So, I am leading this ministry as a full-time endeavor.

It has been a gratifying experience to see God use this model to move congregations and individual believers toward lifestyle ministry, such as those whose stories are given in chapter 1. We do not always recognize God's work. It may be right in front of us, but we miss it because we are not looking with eyes of faith. Yet it has been hard to miss God's hand in the transformational stories shared with me in a dozen years of this ministry. Changed lives and changed churches, as amazing and extraordinary as they are, are not the only evidence of God's hand in the Operation Inasmuch ministry. God has used these experiences to show that he is up to something here that is bigger than any one ministry. Operation Inasmuch is just one tool in his toolbox for renovating the church.

Serve Day (www.serveday.org)

Serve Day is a multi-church experience involving forty congregations in southern California. It is a one-day blitz of believers into the community to assist faith-based, benevolent organizations and to serve people in need. The Web site states the vision of Serve Day as follows: "Our community will be changed by the Christ-following Church working together to demonstrate God's love through acts of empowered kindness and meeting real needs."

Faith in Action

Zondervan, World Vision, and Outreach, Inc. have teamed up to produce the newest model of community ministry: "Faith in Action." This model is a multi-week, comprehensive approach to mobilization of believers into their community, including devotional guides, small group studies, and worship services that climax in one day of community service on a Sunday morning. The model encourages a congregation to cancel their Sunday morning worship and announce to the community they have "Gone Serving."

Unite! (www.uniteus.org)

This is one of several multi-church, citywide models mobilizing believers throughout the Atlanta area. The 2007 version is slated to take place over two days–Saturday and Sunday in October. The Web site lists 120 projects.

Somebody Cares, Tampa Bay! (www.sctb.org)

This is a combined effort among churches, businesses, and community agencies to mobilize many believers in one great day of ministry to people in need. The projects vary from community to community and individuals may volunteer online. This model has been used effectively to bring other cities online in simultaneous days of service.

Reworking Evangelism

God *is* remaking the church. God is slowly but surely transitioning the church from an institution to a mission outpost. God is changing her from a club mentality to an outreach mentality, and not just in evangelism. Church leaders all over the world are rethinking evangelism. They are discovering the inadequacy of traditional methods of evangelism–revivals, door-to-door cold calls, street evangelism, etc. All of these produce some results and we thank God for them, but more and more church leaders are seeing the necessity to earn the right to be heard by our neighbors. That right comes best through service–incarnational ministry, helping people at the point of their need.

Consider this story from Reggie McNeal in *The Present Future:*

Let me tell you my hunch about what effective twenty-first century evangelism will require and what the new apologetic is. I learned it from an experience my wife had a couple of years ago. Cathy went to Ground Zero in November 2001, about two months after the terrorist attacks. She traveled with a disaster relief team of people from our state denomination with a mission to clean apartments of people who had been displaced by the collapse of the World Trade Center. The apartments she cleaned had faced the Twin Towers. All the windows had been blown out when the towers collapsed. These people had watched people jump. They had found telephones, briefcases, jewelry in their apartments all blown in when the towers came crashing down. These residents were paying commercial firms thousands of dollars to get their apartments cleaned. Our team did it for nothing, even leaving gifts behind.

At that time Ground Zero was still a police state. People could come and go only with appropriate identification. Cathy and her team had to wear their disaster relief uniforms so they could get into the area to do their work. These outfits were conspicuous and grabbed people's attention wherever they went. All over Manhattan people stopped them and repeatedly asked three questions: Where are you from? What are you doing? Why? Cathy tells me that by the time they answered the first two questions, "We are from South Carolina, here to clean apartments for people displaced by the terrorist attacks," they could have said anything in response to the "Why?" question and received a hearing. Even if people didn't understand their answer or disagreed with some point of their convictions they were willing to hear them out. Do you know why? They listened because the New Yorkers were persuaded that Cathy and her fellow cleaners believed something so strongly that it had caused them to inconvenience themselves in service to people.

This is what it's going to take to gain a hearing for the gospel in the streets of the twenty-first century–the smell of cleaning solution, dirty faces, obvious acts of servanthood.[8]

Later in his book McNeal tells of another mission trip to New York City involving another member of his family—his daughter. She and her peers went to New York a couple of years after 9/11. They gave out water and took and gave away Polaroid photos and candy in Central Park, but were met with more than a little skepticism and virtually no openness to the gospel. He attributes the differences in experiences between his wife and his daughter to the different approaches to sharing the good news of a loving God. One showed it; the other told it. One authenticated a witness; the other assumed the right to give a witness. As Eric Swanson often says: "Good deeds create good will, becoming a catalyst for good news."[9]

In what has become one of the largest annual gatherings of evangelicals in the nation, the Southern Baptist Convention met in Nashville, Tennessee, in the summer of 2005. They implemented a strategy of evangelism they have dubbed *Crossover*, which they do each year in conjunction with their annual meeting. Hundreds of volunteers are deployed throughout the city where the convention meets in a variety of projects designed to gain opportunities to share a brief witness to the Christian faith to unbelievers. These projects include traditional door-to-door approaches, sports evangelism, block parties, ethnic ministries, focused compassion ministries called "Kindness Explosion," and hard-core street evangelism.

The results of these efforts in 2005 demonstrate the power of compassion ministry to create effective opportunities for evangelism. Of all the persons in the larger Nashville community who responded favorably to these efforts, making decisions to become followers of Jesus, 39 percent came through the compassion ministry projects compared to 22 percent from door-to-door evangelism. The number of people involved in the door-to-door effort, many of whom came from outside Nashville, makes the results even more interesting. There were 7,482 volunteers involved in this humongous effort. They made 18,367 visits and shared the gospel with 5,084 people, with 570 responding with a decision for Christ.[10] While I do not have the total number of volunteers involved in the compassion ministry projects, I have been told by a friend at the Tennessee Baptist Convention who coordinated these projects that far fewer people were involved, yet produced much better results. Upon examination of these results, one leader was heard to comment that they should inform the SBC's future efforts at mass evangelism, and that compassion ministry should receive more attention in the future.

This is just one of many examples of how God is remaking the church through compassion ministry. I suppose one could argue that the public's cynicism about religion and the Christian church in particular has *forced* evangelists to modify their methods. I don't believe that is the case at all. What I have seen is a hunger for authenticity coupled with a fresh wave of compassion in grassroots Christians. I meet them everywhere. There is huge receptivity to the ministry I lead and others described above because of this hunger, which is the work of God's Spirit. When I get to explain to them what Operation Inasmuch can do for their church, I am met by a yearning to see the church ministering effectively to their neighbors. I have done nothing to cultivate that yearning. God is there before me, stirring up the people, opening their eyes to the needs of their neighbors, and convicting them that the God they gather every Sunday to worship truly cares for those people.

All of this is evidence of God's movement to face the church outward. I received an e-mail a few weeks ago from a person I have never met. The sender was a member of a church in eastern Texas. She was writing to tell me her church was preparing to do an Operation Inasmuch in late summer 2007. I replied, asking where she had learned of Operation Inasmuch. She answered that she'd been praying that God would lead her church to reach out to their community better. One day she Googled "community ministry" and ran across our Web site. She went to a bookstore and purchased a copy of the book on Operation Inasmuch, and proceeded to lead her church to use it to reach their community for Christ. Where did this woman's yearning come from? Not from my book or me. I am convinced it came from God.

Missional Churches

The latest "buzz word" in church circles these days is *missional churches*. Books and articles by the score are popping up explaining

how the twenty-first–century church can get back to first-century
thinking or missional thinking. This is not to be confused with a
missions-minded mentality. Milfred Minatrea explains in his book
Shaped by God's Heart:

> "Mission" is…representative; church members pray and
> give so that others may go and serve. Just as churches
> have other programs, such as Christian Education and
> choral music, they also have a missions program. The
> word *missions* is but one expression of the church.
>
> People in the missional church do pray and give
> so that others may go and serve; yet for them *missions*
> is more centered on "being and doing" than "sending
> and supporting." The missional church understands
> that although some may be supported as those sent to
> other locations, every member of the church is "sent."
> Mission is therefore participative rather than simply
> representative.[11]

As I read the literature on missional churches, it seems to me
that God is raising up theologically trained persons to give deeper
thought to what he has been doing with his people. (I can't say if
that is the usual order of God's work–namely, that he leads some
people to act *followed* by theological reflection, but it does seem to
be the case here.) All of the exponents of the missional church say
this is actually the church going back to being incarnational–i.e.,
truly being the embodiment of Christ. This is remembering and
taking as marching orders what Jesus said in Luke 4 when he
spoke in the Nazareth synagogue. This is talking less and doing
more. This is facing the chairs outward and leaving them there.
Ed Stetzer and David Putman say it well:

> A church that is incarnational is interested more in the
> harvest than in the barn. For too long, the church has
> focused on getting the grain into the barn. We have made
> sure the barn is clean, made sure it is attractive, made
> sure it is well organized, and then, we assumed that the
> grains of the wheat would make their way in if we invited
> them. Some did–but most people who could be reached
> that way already have been. Now, it is our job to move

the church from solely attractional methods to engage in missional ones.[12]

The whole body of thought on missional church merely confirms what many have been thinking for some time—namely, that God is at work remaking his church. Whether it is because he has become sufficiently dissatisfied with church as it has become or he is leading his people to find new ways to meet the challenges of the twenty-first century, only he can say. What is certain is that he is up to something. Churches everywhere are awakening to the possibilities of compassion ministry among their neighbors. That this is a movement of God rather than merely a trend is clear to me and to all those I have cited in this chapter. I am praying that the church will listen and follow the Father's leadership.

Some of us are committed to seeing the church's chairs turned around *and nailed to the floor once turned around.* Apparently, Rick Warren is similarly committed. In a sermon at Saddleback Community Church in 2003, he said:

> The bottom line is that we intend to reinvent mission strategy in the 21st century...In the 1st century, mission strategy was always congregationally based... There were no mission societies, mission boards, or parachurch organizations...Today, most local churches are sidelined and uninvolved when it comes to missions. The message from most mission and parachurch organizations to the local church is essentially "Pray, pay, and get out of the way." But in the 21st century, Kay and I intend to help thousands of other local churches to move back to the frontline in missions, in compassion, and in providing the social services that historically the church provided.[13]

Here are a couple of missional churches. Fellowship Bible Church North in Richardson, Texas, conducts "Love Collin County" in their community. Fellowship's small groups take on compassion projects in one day of ministry. In the 2005 event they cleaned a city park, re-roofed a church that serves a poor area, volunteered at a local medical clinic, painted and remodeled at a Boys and Girls Club, did home repairs for elderly persons, volunteered at an abortion alternative clinic, and served at the

City House Shelter. Almost 800 church folk were involved, which is about 40 percent of the total church membership. Pastor Glen Brechner says: "This one day of service is an opportunity to build momentum for bridge-building and launching our small groups into community service. It is also an opportunity to let more people in the church get a taste of community service."[14] When 40 percent of a church's chairs are faced outward, others are sure to follow.

Milfred Minatrea includes in his book the amazing story of New Heights Church in Vancouver, Washington. Out of a concern to support local schools and, through the schools, to meet the needs of some of the students in their community, they came up with a creative way to do that. In Pastor Matt Hannan's own words, here is what they did:

> We made an appointment with one of the school principals. After introducing ourselves we said, "We are here on behalf of the leadership of the New Heights Church. Our folks value what you are doing in educating young people. Frankly we are here to ask you to do [us] a favor. This is a checkbook and you will notice that the account is made out in your name. We have placed $1,000 in the account. We believe that you care for kids, and we care for kids. We want to unite on our common ground.
>
> If we tried, we could probably find a bunch of things over which we would differ, but we don't care about those. We care that you love kids and we love kids. So we are asking you to be our agent in this school. We know you have educational foundation available for certain needs, but we also know it can take a month to get $50 for a pair of shoes for a young person who needs them right now. Besides that, the amount you really needed was more like $75 anyway, but you were limited in the amount you could request.
>
> So, here is a thousand dollars for you to use as needed. We are not asking you to account to us. You are a man of integrity. You will figure out some system to use in caring for the account. If you want to share that with us, that's great, but it is not required. When the amount in the checkbook is getting low, if you will let us know, we will

fill it back up again. We just want to help make it a little easier for you to do what you normally do.[15]

"When we finished talking," Hannan concluded, "there sat this big old principal, just crying like a baby." Hannan shared one result that has emerged from their strategy: "We now have eighteen members of his staff attending New Heights, and initially most of them were not Christians." That's missional. That's a church that shows what can happen when the fresh movement of God washes over a church whose chairs are faced outward.

Have I made my case? Do you see that God is up to something these days and that this something is nothing less than remaking the church? Do you see the role compassion ministry plays in this new (call it missional, or external focus, or whatever you like) movement? A more important question is: What are the implications of this movement for your church, even more so for your life? If God is leading church after church to rediscover the power and value of compassion ministry, what does it say about how you can invest yourself? How you answer these questions will determine whether you are ready to take up a lifestyle of compassion ministry.

Notes

[1]Reggie McNeal, *The Present Future: Six Tough Questions for the Church* (San Francisco: Jossey-Bass, 2003), 43.

[2]Ibid., 44.

[3]Alexandra McNabb, "Widening the Funnel in Externally Focused Churches," an article posted on the Web site of Leadership Network, www.leadnet.org, 1.

[4]From www.sharefest.org, "History" page.

[5]From www.kingdomassignment.com/gettingstarted.

[6]From www.justfaith.org, "History" page.

[7]David Crocker, *Operation Inasmuch: Mobilizing Believers beyond the Walls of the Church* (St. Louis: Chalice Press, 2005).

[8]McNeal, *The Present Future*, 37–38.

[9]Eric Swanson, www.leadnet.org. Home page.

[10]These statistics are from unpublished reports of the North American Mission Board of the Southern Baptist Convention, 2005.

[11]Milfred Minatrea, *Shaped by God's Heart: The Passion and Practices of Missional Churches* (San Francisco: Jossey-Bass, 2004), 10–11.

[12]Ed Stetzer and David Putman, *Breaking the Missional Code* (Nashville: Broadman & Holman, 2006), 65.

[13]Rick Warren, www.saddlebackfamily.com/peace/Services, cited in ibid., 173–74.

[14]Glen Brechner, quoted in Krista Petty, "Six Catalytic Service Approaches," posted on the Leadership Network Web site, www.leadnet.org.

[15]Matt Hannan, quoted in Minatrea, *Shaped by God's Heart*, 95–96.

7

Moving Down the Funnel

"He gave justice and help to the poor and needy,
  and everything went well for him.
Isn't that what it means to know me?"
  says the LORD.

JEREMIAH 22:16 (NLT)

*For we are God's masterpiece. He created us anew in Christ
Jesus so that we can do the good things he planned for us long
ago.*

EPHESIANS 2:10 (NLT)

"Small things done with great love will change the world" is the
mantra of Vineyard Church in Cincinnati, Ohio. The opening line
of the "About Us" page on the Servant Evangelism Web site (www.
servantevangelism.com) says: "Perhaps our motto should read,
'Small Things Done with Great Love Are Changing the World'
because that's what's happening. We get reports from pastors,
lay leaders and ordinary Christ-followers all over the world who
have discovered the power and impact of showing God's love in
practical ways."[1]

I would modify this saying to say: "Small things done with
great love *are* changing the *church.*" Sometimes a decision or action
taken by church leaders, when inspired by God and blessed by
him, moves a church in an entirely different direction. Such was

116

the case for Mariners Church in Irvine, California. Mariners is one of the premier role models for compassion ministry in the world. In the fiscal year 2006–2007 ending June 30, Mariners had 4,683 people involved in ongoing community ministry throughout their community out of an average weekend attendance of about 8,000. *That means 58.5 percent of their active membership is doing lifestyle compassion ministry.*

Of course, Mariners did not begin with more than half of their church involved in compassion ministry. As is often the case, they began small–with a decision by Senior Pastor Kenton Beshore to share excess funds with benevolent nonprofits in the larger community where Mariners is located. (A spiritual principle at work here needs to be highlighted before continuing with the Mariner's story–namely, that whenever we do what God tells us to do, he *always* has something more in mind. I have seen this principle verified time and time again, so much so that it is my own personal motto for life.)

When Beshore accepted the role of senior pastor of Mariners Church, it was with the understanding that the church would not end the year in the red. At the end of that first year, sure enough, church finances lagged behind their budget goals. Pastor Beshore challenged the elders to remember his agreement with them and to pray for a solution to their needs. The elders went behind closed doors and did just that. When they emerged, the church coffers not only met their budget but exceeded it by $10,000. Instead of padding the church's accounts, Beshore asked that the excess funds be given to area nonprofits serving the poor.

When this matter was announced to the congregation, a number of people stepped up to say they would be willing to serve on a task force to seek God's leadership in how the church could minister effectively to people in need. After a full year of prayer and monthly, comprehensive study of Scripture, the group shared with the full congregation that God clearly expects his people to minister to *all* people in need, and that Mariners should make that a core value of the church. In response to the group's report, the congregation received a special offering in which another $10,000 was given. Again, these funds were given to area nonprofits and the church followed with partnerships with these organizations. As more Mariners members became personally involved in these ministries, God raised up individuals to start and lead ministries for which the church accepted total responsibility. Within a half-dozen years, Lighthouse Ministries was formed as a major and distinct division of church life. These events served to reengineer the DNA of Mariners. They became the benchmark events and decisions that led to the development of some of the most impressive community ministries of any church in America.

Mariners' stable of compassion ministries includes a wide variety of local community ministries. CAMPS provide a summer camp experience for at-risk youth. Foster Care and Adoption includes special events for children in protective custody, ministry to children in foster care, preparation for families to become foster or adoptive parents, and mentoring ministries. The Lighthouse Community Center meets the needs of families living in the high-risk area of Santa Ana for three age groups: children, teens, and adults. Miracles in Motion ministers to families living in motels in the Costa Mesa area through children's activities, limited food distribution, and relational servant evangelism. Mariners Resource Center accepts tangible donations, which in turn are either given to people or families in need or sold to generate funding for the church's community ministries. The car ministry receives and repairs cars to be given to people without transportation.

Additionally, Mariners provides these opportunities for compassion ministry:

- *Psalm 139:* provides encouragement to pregnant teens in local shelters
- *Club Mom:* support group for pregnant and parenting teens
- *FamilyWorks:* provides hope and resources to families in need
- *Habitat for Humanity:* works with the local chapter of Habitat to build new homes for the working poor
- *House of Hope:* brings hope to previously homeless women and their children
- *Joy Carriers:* visits seniors in assisted living facilities
- *Spa Days:* hosts days of pampering for women served by Lighthouse Ministries
- *Military Support Ministry:* offers various kinds of support to military personnel and their families

- *HopeBuilders:* improves living conditions for families in substandard housing

The Funnel

As with other churches that have developed a culture of compassion ministry, Mariners has used the image of a funnel to portray the process of moving Christ-followers into lifestyle compassion ministry. The purpose of a funnel is to facilitate moving something into a small space to serve a specific purpose–a quart of oil from its container into the crankcase of a lawnmower, salt from a one-pound box into a small saltshaker, and people from an unfocused, "it's-about-us" mentality into a lifestyle of compassion ministry. The top of the funnel is wide to make it as easy as possible to move something into it without making a mess. The bottom of the funnel is narrow to get what we are pouring where we want it.

The bottom of the funnel is where we want to see people go. The goal is lifestyle compassion ministry, or–as shown in the figure on page 121–serving regularly from a high commitment to compassion ministry, experiencing a change in priorities, and mobilizing others.

Some believers move themselves into lifestyle compassion ministry. They quickly process what has just happened to them– that they found meaning and satisfaction in their one-day of ministry–and they want more. The Kim Kincers or Marie Clowers in the church do not wait for church leaders to guide them into ongoing compassion ministry; they initiate their own. In my first book, I told about Sandy Spaugh, a member of Ardmore Baptist Church, Winston-Salem, North Carolina. Sandy was a member of a crew of volunteers who reworked the playground of an elementary school. The school population is primarily poor children and, consequently, it often is neglected by the local school system. After her day of sloshing around with friends in the mud at Latham Elementary School, it occurred to Sandy that some of the children at the school might need some help with reading. She sought out the principal and volunteered. In her own words:

> I decided to reach out to Latham Elementary School and see if they would accept me as a reading tutor for a few

children. Each day from 1:00 to 3:00 I had four third-grade children who formed a circle and read with me. When the children complained that what we were reading was boring, I wrote stories of my own, stories about what it was like in the old days when I was a kid. They could not wait for the next story. I put them together to form a book and gave each child a copy. We took field trips to places in the book—my childhood home, the stores where I shopped as a child, the school I attended (now a church). The children drew the pictures to illustrate the stories I wrote and they are included in my book.[2]

Sandy found her ministry with those children. She quickly moved down the funnel from an Operation Inasmuch to her own compassion ministry. Unfortunately, this sort of thing is the exception, not the rule. Not many church folk initiate their own compassion ministry after one day of community ministry with fellow members. Most need help doing that, hence the purpose of this book, and this chapter in particular. As if there is a sieve just an inch below the top of the funnel, they get stuck there and never get to the bottom in lifestyle ministry. Even if they participate in other days of ministry or short-term mission trips, that experience never quite becomes part of their routine life. They step out of their routines to do one day of ministry or a short-term trip, then step back into their lives, which do not have compassion ministry as part of them.

The top of the funnel of compassion ministry is an opportunity to get involved in a safe, low-investment ministry.[3] It offers people the chance to get their feet wet in ministry. It requires little time or preparation and very little commitment. It takes seriously their concerns about doing something they may never have done before. Serve Day and Operation Inasmuch are examples of top-of-the-funnel opportunities in compassion ministry. People participate for a day (often just a few hours) in hands-on ministry projects such as painting a school, or working at a homeless shelter, or building a wheelchair ramp for a disabled homeowner. When they leave at the end of the day, they have no other responsibility for that project, or any other similar project. *However,* they have taken a step out of their comfort zones and tasted the joy of serving others in Jesus' name. More often than not, they find their day of service to be meaningful and enjoyable. Ministering to others without regard for reward produces its own rewards.

PROCESS FOR LIFESTYLE COMPASSION MINISTRY

Take a closer look at each level of the funnel. (Mariners Church actually adds more "E's" to their funnel: *Expose, Enfold, Engage, Equip,* and *Empower. Enfold* is a question a ministry leader is urged to ask: How many people choose to take next steps in my ministry? *Equip* refers to a ministry leader's training of the volunteers in his/her care: How many people am I training in the vision, values, and skills of my ministry?)

Expose

Wise church leaders recognize that change comes slowly in believers. As impressive as stories of dramatic change may be, and we have all heard them, they are the exception. For most of us change is a slow process. Movement toward compassion ministry begins with exposure to it in a low-commitment, low-cost opportunity to serve. If we provide an opportunity for people to experience some of the benefits of serving without asking them for the sort of commitment that requires wholesale changes in their lives, there is a better chance they will respond favorably. Once they have tasted the joy of serving, they are more willing to take another step. The chart below gives graphic expression to this process.[4]

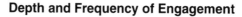
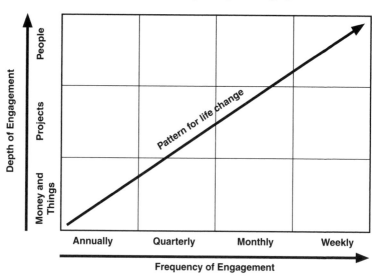

Depth and Frequency of Engagement

This chart shows that life change comes with frequency of involvement and depth of engagement—from money to time to people. Life change is what this book is about, moving believers closer to authentic discipleship through compassion ministry. A second chart below shows this process in greater depth.[5]

As with the first chart, as duration and complexity increase, so does life change. This chart also shows the greater impact a person involved in lifestyle compassion ministry has on his or her community. Basic assistance and short-term projects are top-of-the-funnel activities. They expose a believer to compassion ministry. I would not include monetary donations in this phase. Giving money, in most cases, requires very little thought or commitment and can hardly be considered an activity that leads toward change, which is why "Monetary donations" is listed in the bottom left of the chart.

What the mid-section of this chart shows—intermediate activities and long-term, mutual transformation such as mentoring—are lifestyle compassion ministries. They represent what lifestyle

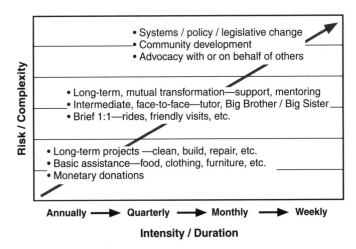

compassion ministry looks like. The activities at the top right of the chart represent further developments or results of persons' involvement in lifestyle compassion ministry. Mike Moser and Sue Byrd, whose stories are told in chapter 1, are examples of this level of involvement. This level is beyond the *Engage* phase of the lifestyle compassion ministry funnel. It is similar to one's calling to serve as a professional or vocational minister as compared to the call for all believers to follow Jesus in every aspect of their daily lives. This is not to say that a person cannot be involved in advocacy or policy change without such a calling. It simply acknowledges the reality that involvement at this level goes beyond what I have described in this book as lifestyle compassion ministry.

Experience

Now look at the funnel again. People who move down the funnel from *Exposure* to *Experience* have reflected on their exposure to compassion ministry sufficiently to know that they want more. Whether or not such people understand totally the value of this sort of ministry (most people certainly do *not* have a thorough theology of compassion ministry at this point), they acknowledge that serving others in Jesus' name is fulfilling, so that such people are willing to give more of themselves. Behavior changes first, followed by values and priorities.

Mariners is intentional about moving people down the funnel into the *Experience* phase of involvement. Ministry leaders observe volunteers in their first-step experiences in compassion ministry. They intentionally leave themselves free from administrative details during a ministry event so as to be able to "read" the volunteers. Within two weeks after an event, they communicate, in a letter, their gratitude for a person's involvement and invite the person to consider taking another step. This invitation is often expressed in something along these lines: "We have a need for (*a specific community ministry need*). Would you pray about helping us meet that need?" The person is not asked to make a lifestyle change at this point, only to take another step to see of this kind of ministry "fits" him or her. If the person does not accept this invitation, the church offers another one at another time. Through nearly twenty years of conducting and refining compassion ministry, Mariners' leaders have developed a healthy respect for the different ways individuals process opportunities to serve. The leaders do not push or cajole, but rather allow persons to advance at their own pace.

Engage

Movement down the funnel from *Experience* to *Engage* takes time. According to the leaders at Mariners, it may take a year or two to move beyond the ministry events that require lower commitment. However, some people never reach the next level. I visited Mariners to learn how they do compassion ministry. A statement given in one of my conversations with leaders at the church reveals their wisdom in giving individuals the responsibility and freedom to move down the funnel at their own pace. Kelly McFadden said: "God calls us to give people opportunities to serve people in need. It is his job to change hearts."

And that is precisely what God is doing at Mariners. In the September-November issue of their *Lighthouse* newsletter, the following story illustrates just how Mariners folk move from first-step opportunities to serve more fully in lifestyle compassion ministry:

> I was first introduced to the Miracles in Motion ministry a couple of years ago through someone I knew in the singles ministry. She was looking for volunteers to come serve with her at the Fall Carnival. Not knowing exactly what was involved, I showed up that Saturday and helped wherever I was needed. I then signed up to help with

the Thanksgiving dinner that same year, just feeling like I wanted to give the residents something to be thankful for. Little did I know, God was softening my heart toward those living at the motel.

The summer of 2006 is when I began to feel God tugging at my heart to become more involved. I showed up at a monthly birthday party at the motel and found myself loving the opportunity to serve so much I decided to commit myself to serving in a larger capacity. I now regularly serve at most of the main events; I served for the first time at MiM Camp a couple of weeks ago, and am an active member of the Prayer Team.

Through this ministry God has taught me to look outside myself. He has given me compassion for those that have so little. I want to share with them about Christ and his love for them. I want to let them know there is hope in him, no matter what their situation. Serving has helped me take my eyes off of myself and my selfish desires. It has shown me how to focus on his Kingdom and his purpose to seek and save the lost.[6]

Tips for Making Compassion Ministry Part of Your DNA

Before moving on to the steps a congregation can take to move people down the funnel, I want to share more of what I learned in my visit to Mariners Church. The church has honed its processes to such a point that it would be foolish not to glean all the learnings possible from it. There are several things they do that give systemic support to the value of lifestyle compassion ministry. First, they track all volunteer involvement—not only in all of the Lighthouse Ministries, but also in their global ministries. They record and measure every person's involvement whether volunteer or leader, including each time the person serves and the hours served. A full-time staff person has as her primary role to maintain this tracking system. At the end of their fiscal year, they produce reports similar to end-of-year financial reports. More importantly, they give these reports the prominence most churches give their financial reports.

Mariners uses these metrics as the basis for budget and program plans each year. They also use them as a primary source of each ministry leader's effectiveness. Performance appraisals draw heavily from these metrics. Every leader, whether volunteer or paid staff, is expected to "hit his or her marks" in terms of the numbers of people involved in that ministry and the number who have taken next steps to move down the funnel. I know what you're thinking, and the answer is "yes"–they have occasionally asked ministry leaders to step down when they consistently fail to produce results or, in some cases, fail to provide the metrics required from their ministries.

When I asked why Mariners attaches so much importance to tracking ministry involvement, I was told that they have found that they cannot possibly know the effectiveness of their ministries without them. They cannot know which ministries are working well–and, therefore, which ones in which to invest more heavily and which to dissolve–without reliable metrics. I was told, "It's a matter of stewardship." Wanting to make the best possible use of the resources God has provided them, leaders at Mariners are serious about tracking their constituents' involvement in compassion ministry.

Leaders at Mariners have learned that God does a better job of raising up ministries and ministry leaders than they do. In my conversations with them, I was told over and over that it is not the job of the Lighthouse Ministry team to develop new ministries, although they are totally open to new ministry opportunities to meet the demand of a growing church membership and ever-increasing movement toward lifestyle compassion ministry. Rather, they depend on individuals to respond to God's urging to meet a need. If these individuals believe God is leading to a more developed ministry for that need, the church will come alongside them to develop such a ministry. Mariners calls these individuals "champions." They champion a ministry until it becomes part of the stable of Lighthouse Ministries.

Miracles in Motion ministries began just this way. An individual conducted a study of the local population who live in motels and was shocked at what she found. She felt she should do something to help these people, so she began going to one of the motels regularly to do what she could to minister to the residents in Jesus' name. When the needs became more than she could meet, she invited her friends to help. Eventually, the church took on "her" motel as one of its ministry points. Today, more than six hundred volunteers get involved each year in all the Miracles in Motion ministries.

Another reinforcement of the value Mariners places on compassion ministry is its Lighthouse Weekend, which takes place each fall. This event celebrates and promotes local ministries. The worship times for the weekend focus on the Lighthouse Ministries. People tell stories about how God is using these ministries to transform people—Mariners constituents as well as many of their neighbors in need. In these worship times, they receive an offering just for the Lighthouse Ministries. And here is what's special about this—they pass offering baskets to receive this offering. It is policy at Mariners that they do not pass offering baskets or plates in any of their worship services. Instead, they have attractive offering boxes at the exits of the worship center and encourage people to deposit their tithes and offerings there. They do this because they know that one of the primary objections unchurched people have about church is that it is mostly interested in getting their money. *The one time Mariners departs from this policy is to support their efforts at compassion ministry.* Does that say how important they believe these ministries are, or what? Incidentally, the Lighthouse Ministries receives no funding through the operating budget of the church, but rather relies on this special offering on Lighthouse Weekend and special gifts given to the ministry throughout the year.

Through years of moving people down the funnel of compassion ministry, leaders at Mariners have identified the barriers to this movement. Congregational leaders wanting to lead their people into lifestyle compassion ministry would be wise to know what these barriers are. Probably the most prominent is fear—fear of the ministry environment if the location is a place that is less safe than volunteers are accustomed to, fear of the discomfort that stems from facing real need, and fear from simply having to move out of one's comfort zone. Also, limited resources always hinder compassion ministry. There are always more needs than even the most resourceful and affluent congregation can meet when they get serious about meeting the needs of their community.

An entitlement attitude on the part of the recipients can be a barrier to compassion ministry. Often recipients have learned to depend on the help of others, either government or nonprofits, and expect it. When they communicate this expectation to volunteers, it can produce resentment in those volunteers and, if not dealt with adequately, can lead to a resistance to greater involvement. The attitude of managers or leaders of nonprofits or organizations with whom churches partner to do compassion ministry can be a problem as well. As an example, Mariners' Miracles in Motion ministry to the resident motel population has often had to work around an uncooperative attitude of the motel manager to render their ministry.

Finally, policies and procedures of compassion ministries may be perceived as barriers to volunteers. Sometimes volunteers approach such ministry with the attitude: I am giving my time to do this ministry; I should be allowed to do it as I see fit. However, experienced ministry leaders have learned over time the best ways of conducting ministry in their particular contexts. Helping volunteers understand the time-tested policies and procedures can seem like an unnecessary bother, but it always proves to be a wise investment of a leader's time.

The Decision

Believers move beyond the in-and-out experience with compassion ministry when their church provides a compelling picture of lifestyle compassion ministry and a means to get there. As a pastor for twenty-five years, I can tell you that very little gets done in a church without clear decisions that move the church forward. Of course, God can do amazing things with churches, but he usually does not do so without the cooperation of the leaders and the people. So a decision—somehow, some way, some time—to move toward lifestyle compassion ministry is necessary to get there. It is best when this decision comes as a result of prayerful reflection and seeking God's face as in the case of Mariner's Church.

Individual believers *can* be involved in lifestyle compassion ministry without their churches deciding to move in that direction as a congregation. Without a doubt, God has called out many individuals to serve people in need as a lifestyle with hardly anyone in their churches being aware, much less approving. I have met many of these folk in my travels around the country. They inspire me and keep me going. Unfortunately, their number is small.

Churches can see many more of their constituents move down the funnel when the churches give lifestyle compassion ministry priority through clear, prayed-through, God-led decisions.

If you are a pastor or congregational leader, you may cringe a little at this suggestion because you know there will be resistance. It will require people to move from their comfort zone into a new realm of life. It will demand their time, energy, creativity, and, maybe, their money. So, you will have to be wise, even cunning, but that's nothing new. You know how to get things done in your church: get the right people involved, feed them all the information and encouragement you can, and get out of the way! *But don't stop until you have a decision to move folks into a lifestyle of compassion ministry!* Without that decision, it will not happen. Be patient. Be wise. But be persistent until you have it. You will be glad you did.

As for steps to be taken in obtaining this decision, help can be found in resources such as the books and Web sites cited in this book. The Externally Focused Churches portion of the Leadership Network site offers several insightful (and downloadable) articles, primarily "Widening the Funnel in Externally Focused Churches." I will summarize the article here but I encourage you to download it, print it off and circulate it among your leadership team. This is part of the information you need to feed a steady stream to your team.

Prayer

It all begins with prayer. This is especially true for churches in which traditions run deep and change comes slowly. These are the churches referenced in chapter 3, in which the "it's-about-us" mentality prevails, and, therefore, offers stiff resistance to any idea of diverting attention and resources away from the "club" to those in the community. Author Richard Foster's definition of prayer fits here: "To pray is to change." To pray is to align our desires, passions, and dreams with God's, and that always leads to change, whether dramatic or incremental. Prayer puts us in touch with God's heart, and when prayer is grounded in humility, it exposes us to God's priority for the poor and oppressed. Remember that Jesus spent forty days in the wilderness praying and fasting *before* he launched his public ministry.

As reported above, prayer played a significant role in the transformation of Mariners Church. Another example comes from Pastor Rick McKinley of Imago Dei, Portland, Oregon. He says about the starting point of prayer for compassion ministry:

> There must be a paradigm shift in the church from "It's for me" to "It's for them," and "serve us," versus "service." We began with pretty skeptical believers because the evangelism card is thrown down so often–loving people as an ulterior motive. And believers are not taught or shown that the gospel can really transform people. We had to begin by asking God for a changed heart to repent of sins of omission–the things we were not doing and did not want to do for the people of the city."[7]

Vision

Concurrent with a church-wide emphasis on prayer to seek God's will for the church in terms of its relationship with the community, it is wise to cast a vision of compassion ministry. The following words of Antoine de Saint-Exupery say volumes about the power of vision:

> If you want to build a ship, don't drum up the men to gather wood, divide the work, and give orders. Instead, teach them to yearn for the vast and endless sea.[8]

The plain fact is that most people are drawn to God-sized visions. They inspire and motivate like nothing else. Think of Abraham Lincoln's charge to "bind up the nation's wounds," Winston Churchill's rallying "This was their finest hour," John Kennedy's challenge to the country to send a man to the moon and return him safely before the end of the decade. Before our church folk will move down the funnel of compassion ministry, they need to have a vision of what that is like. Lifestyle compassion ministry is a significant change for most people, and significant change *never* comes without vision. There are three ways to cast a vision for lifestyle compassion ministry.

Tell the Biblical Story of God's Heart for the Poor

The biblical story ought always to inform and inspire our visions of Kingdom life. We believe the Bible. We take our "marching orders" from the Bible. So, we should allow the Bible to inform us concerning God's heart for the poor. As a pastor, I enjoyed casting a vision. I loved talking about God's purposes for the church, holding high his shaping of the church to do his work. I found that God's vision *always* evokes some sort of response. It's not the sort of thing one can be neutral about. Either you are moved by it to make changes in your life (or in the church) or you resist it because you are afraid of what it will cost you, but neutrality is not an option. Congregational leaders cast vision all the time—for capital stewardship campaigns, for strategic plans, etc. Vision casting is just as essential for compassion ministry.

This is born out in the experience of Mariners Church. As their task force immersed themselves in a comprehensive study of what God says in his Word about caring for the poor and marginalized, they came face-to-face with incontrovertible evidence that such ministry must be a priority of God's people. The power of the Word should never be underestimated.

Tell Stories of Churches with a Culture of Compassion Ministry

I have said it before and I say it again: *story* is powerful. Good stories draw us in. They stimulate the use of imagination, which includes finding our place in them. Stories about churches that have developed a culture of compassion ministry, such as the story of Mariners Church given at the beginning of this chapter, are compelling. When we hear them, we can't help thinking: *If they can do it, we can too.* The books and Web sites cited in this book will supply a stream of positive stories about compassion-driven, externally focused congregations. They show what God is doing to face congregations outward toward their communities, and any time we talk about what God is doing, people are inspired and motivated.

Invite congregational leaders from those churches to share with your congregation. Show videos that tell stories of this sort of transformation, especially if they include a before-and-after aspect. Most people who are being challenged to consider significant change find encouragement in others' struggles with those same changes.

Purchase multiple copies of books about churches being externally focused and ask people to read them. Then gather them together to talk about the book and its implications for their church. I have done this with some success. It is surprising what simple exposure to different ideas and new ways of doing church can do to stimulate new thinking, even new visions of what can be.

Tell Stories of Individual Believers Who Have Taken Up a Lifestyle of Compassion Ministry

Better yet, have them tell their own stories. Invite people who have already made the transition to lifestyle compassion ministry to tell about their journeys. Import them if you have to, inviting them from other churches, even from outside your own community if necessary. Mariners Church has made storytelling part of what it calls its "tool belt," which is a small brochure spelling out its vision and core values as a church. Mariners refers constantly to maintaining the course it believes God has given it. The Lighthouse newsletter mentioned above is a collection of stories from Mariners members who are involved.

Each Tuesday morning, the entire ministry team at Mariners meet for "Story Time." Senior Pastor Kenton Beshore leads in a brief devotion, then he hands off the microphone to any staff member who has a story to tell. There is never a shortage of people willing to share. Many of the stories related at "Story Time" come from the Lighthouse Ministries. Consequently, the ministry team is constantly energized about their work and inspired to expand it, because they are always hearing how lives are being transformed.

When I visited Mariners and learned how they use storytelling to keep their vision of ministry to people in need in front of them all the time, I asked how they capture stories of God using their ministries to transform people. I was given a copy of the guidelines some ministry leaders use to help their volunteers know how to tell their stories. In keeping with the spirit of this book in offering tips to help you move people down the funnel, I give you below the points of Mariners' "Elements of a Great Story."[9]

- *First, identify the audience* and design the *purpose* of the story *to that audience.* How do you tell the story best to that audience?
- *Next, state the purpose* of the story *up front—why* you're telling this story. Example: "One of the values we have at our

church is…," or, "I'm going to tell you a story about how God…"

- Use brief key *background,* connecting statements (when necessary) so they can connect with your story.
- *Write the story with emotion.* Be comfortable with your emotions. Don't apologize or fight them back. Take a deep breath and say: "This is emotional for me," or, "This is really powerful for me."
- *Write why it's emotional.* "It's emotional because…" It paints a beautiful picture, allowing people to really connect with the story.
- Needs to be *authentic.* People can see when it isn't and it hurts the story.
- It is okay to tell a story *without an ending.* It still tells well. ("We will see what God is still going to do.")
- Good stories tend to *meander;* they never happen in a straight line.
- *Too much detail* can *kill a great story.* Be *selective* or it will take away from the story.
- After the first draft, ask yourself, *"Does it tell?"* "Is there a better way to tell this?"

I say it again: the bottom of the funnel is where we want people to be. We want them to follow Jesus by making ministry to people in need a lifestyle. *God wants them to show the poor and marginalized that he loves them.* He wants all of us who are followers of Jesus to carry on the ministry of Jesus in all its facets, including help for people in need.

If you are a believer who has tasted the challenges and rewards of compassion ministry but have not yet made it a lifestyle, why not take the next step? Why not accept your experiences in compassion ministry as God's invitation to do more? Why not move down the funnel?

If you are a congregational leader whose church has offered top-of-the-funnel ministry opportunities to your congregation but have not yet developed ways to help those who are willing to move down the funnel, why not take the next step? Why not implement some of the ideas and procedures offered in this chapter in your church? Why not challenge your church to become a Good Samaritan church?

Notes

[1]From www.servantevangelism.com.

[2]Letter from Sandy Spaugh, February 1, 2000.

[3]The funnel graphic shown on page 121 appears in "Widening the Funnel in Externally Focused Churches," an article by Alexandra McNabb posted on the Leadership Network, www.leadnet.org.

[4]Illustration by Eric Swanson in ibid.

[5]Source unknown.

[6]Cindy Sanchez, "Where Hope Is Found," *Lighthouse,* the Mariners Church newsletter (September/October/November, 2007): 3.

[7]Rick McKinley, quoted in McNabb, "Widening the Funnel in Externally Focused Churches."

[8]Antoine de Saint-Exupery, as quoted in Milfred Minatrea, *Shaped by God's Heart: The Passion and Practices of Missional Churches* (San Francisco: Jossey-Bass, 2004), xvii.

[9]These guidelines are not published but were shared with the author.

8

Churches That Make
a Difference

Culture is to the church what a soul is to the human body. It is an overall life force that the Holy Spirit uses to give energy, personality, and uniqueness to everything a body of believers says and does.

ROBERT LEWIS AND WAYNE CORDEIRO

Having been a pastor for twenty-five years, I developed the habit of always being in a gathering mode: gathering stories, facts, quotes, and ideas I could use in preaching. One piece I gathered is a humorous take on change and the church. It asks, "How many _____ does it take to change a light bulb?" and fills in the blank with persons of various denominations and ministerial roles. It goes like this:

- How many youth ministers does it take to change a light bulb? Answer: Youth ministers aren't around long enough for a light bulb to burn out.
- How many Amish does it take to change a light bulb? Answer: What's a light bulb?
- How many independent fundamentalists does it take to change a light bulb? Answer: Only one, because any more might result in too much cooperation.

135

My favorite is: "How many Southern Baptists does it take to change a light bulb?" Answer: 109. Five on the Light Bulb Task Force Subcommittee, who report to the ten on the Light Bulb Task Force, appointed by the twelve on the Trustee Board. Their recommendation is reviewed by the Executive Finance Committee of five, who place it on the agenda of the sixteen-member Finance Committee. If they approve, they bring a motion to the twenty-four-member Church Board, who appoint another committee of nine to schedule the changing of the light bulb with the administrator, who reports to the fifteen-member Personnel Committee, who reviews the janitor's job description to make sure light bulb changing is included there, then pass the matter on to the Maintenance Committee to purchase a light bulb, who has to submit a requisition to the Finance Secretary for the purchase. By the time all this is done, no one can remember which light bulb needed changing.

You get the point. Bureaucracy, tradition, and plain old stubbornness make it hard for churches to change. Yet, change they must...*IF* they are to fulfill their calling. Not all churches understand that, and, if we are to believe what we are told about how many churches in the country die every week, that number is very high. On the other hand, a growing segment of churches get it–not all the members of these churches, to be sure, but enough that there is reason to believe they just might make the transitions necessary not simply to survive but to become a force for Christ in their communities. These are the churches that are looking for positive models. The leaders of these churches are the folk who are still reading this book hoping to clarify their still-fuzzy vision of what it means to be a church with a culture of compassion ministry.

This is precisely what I hope to accomplish in this chapter: provide a clear picture of a culture of compassion ministry at work in the local church. First, I offer some ways of understanding church culture. Second, I identify the primary characteristics of churches with a culture of compassion ministry. Third, and most importantly, I hold up a couple of models for you to see–examples of congregations who have transitioned from a status quo, business-as-usual, traditional church to a vibrant, externally focused, compassion-driven church.

What Is Church Culture?

Culture is totally pervasive. It is the way people in a particular context behave without thinking about it, the way they think without being aware of it. Culture goes beyond traditions. Culture is all-encompassing, having to do with values and beliefs. Robert Lewis of Fellowship Bible Church, Little Rock, Arkansas, and Wayne Cordeiro of New Hope Christian Fellowship, Honolulu, Hawaii, teamed up a couple of years ago to write a much-needed guide to understanding and transforming church culture in *Culture Shift: Transforming Your Church from the Inside Out.* They state up-front what most church leaders have known at some level, but may not have fully understood:

> Culture is the most important social reality in your church. Though invisible to the untrained eye, its power is undeniable. Culture gives color and flavor to everything your church is and does. Like a powerful current running through your church, it can move you inland or take you farther out to sea. It can prevent your church's potential from ever being realized, or—if used by the Holy Spirit—it can draw others in and reproduce healthy spiritual life all along the way.[1]

You may be thinking: *Yeah, I suspected something like that, but how do I determine what the culture of my church is?* Lewis and Cordeiro offer a simple, commonsense process for doing just that, and since my goal for this book is to encourage churches to develop a culture of compassion ministry, I pass on their process here.[2]

1. Look at leadership and values: Who are the culture setters in your church? Are they the elected leaders or are they unelected but highly influential? Is your leadership team on the same page in the values they espouse and practice? What are the real (not necessarily the stated) values of the church? What values does the community impose on the church from its history and traditions?
2. Look at the vision statement of your church: Is the church's vision stated in a succinct, serious, written document that leaders and the congregation know and embrace? Is the vision statement consistent with activities?

3. Look at your symbols, ceremonies, and celebrations: What are your church's symbols or totems–those things that have powerful stories associated with them? What are the ceremonies and rituals honored in your church? Who are the heroes?

4. Look at yourself as a leader: This applies to lay leaders as well as professional ministers. What do you really value? What are your success indicators? What drives you especially when the going gets rough? When was the last time you took a risk and why?

Identifying your church's culture will take a great deal of time and energy. You will have to be totally committed to completing the task, but it will prove enormously, beneficial leading your church toward a culture of compassion ministry. Unless your church already has such a culture, your examination of your church's culture will lead to some revelations that just may rock you. But don't dismay. Being the church Jesus called us to be has never been easy. Your battles have been fought thousands, even millions of times, and God is still in the transformation business.

A Culture of Compassion Ministry

I use the term *culture* here to describe the desired environment in a church in which its members and visitors go about being church in a particular way. What way? This way:

- They embrace and practice what it means to be truly externally focused.
- Significant numbers of them are deployed throughout their community in compassion ministries.
- They often use terms such as *compassion* or *serving the community* or *focused outward* to describe their church to others.
- Their community knows them as people who care about the larger community.
- Compassion ministry influences their decision-making.
- People are attracted to them, and some actually begin attending, because of their compassion ministry.

Let's drill down on each of these characteristics a bit.

They embrace and practice what it means to be truly externally focused.
In their superb book *Externally Focused Churches*, Rick Rusaw and Eric
Swanson list the characteristics of externally focused churches:

- They are convinced that good deeds and good news cannot
  and should not be separated.
- They see themselves as vital to the health and well-being
  of their communities.
- They believe that ministering and serving are the normal
  expressions of Christian living.
- They are evangelistically effective.[3]

Externally focused churches understand that the church is the
one organization in the community that does not exist primary for
its own well-being but for those not of its number. These churches
target most of their ministries not at their own members but at
their neighbors. When asked to list the disciplines of the Christian
life, they identify service for others, perhaps even caring for the
poor, among the top five. They see ministry as the primary and
the most effective way to share the good news of God's love with
those who have not experienced it. Evangelism is not an ulterior
motive, but rather the *ultimate* motive, for ministry. Churches
with a culture of compassion ministry have turned their chairs
around and left them that way. Describing such churches, Rusaw
and Swanson say:

> Pastors and Christian leaders all around the world are
> beginning to think differently about church. Independently
> of one another, they are increasingly convinced that
> effectiveness is not measured by what happens inside the
> church but rather by the impact the people of the church
> have on their communities.[4]

Swanson's own church is an excellent example of what he and
Rusaw mean by externally focused churches. When they were
faced with expanding their facilities because of their growth, they
did not simply develop ideas and plans based on the congregation's
wishes, but invited groups from the community—school personnel,
city officials, civic organizations—to suggest how the church's new
facilities could service the community. That's externally focused
thinking, and it betrays a culture of compassion ministry.

   Significant numbers of church members are deployed throughout their community in compassion ministries. As I stated in an earlier chapter, almost all churches are doing compassion ministries in some manner, albeit in a fragmented, sketchy way. However, a church with a compassion ministry culture is one in which most of its members are involved in ministries beyond the structures of the church. These ministries are for the benefit of persons not associated with the church.

   One of the reasons church leaders resist the notion of deploying lots of their people into the community to staff and serve in various compassion ministries is that it will likely reduce their availability to staff all the volunteer positions in the church. But in a church culture of compassion ministry, leaders *affirm* their people who give themselves in such ministries. They write about them in the church newsletter and Web page. They tell their stories in sermons and other lessons. They brag to their peers about how God is using their people to bless the community.

   In a church culture of compassion ministry, there are structures to encourage and empower members' involvement beyond the walls of the church. I visited one church in the town where I live that held a Community Impact Fair one Sunday. Before, after, and between worship services and Sunday School, members were urged to go to the gymnasium where a couple dozen faith-based ministries were set up to tell what they do and sign up volunteers from the church to participate. The members did not serve that day, but volunteered to serve at another time. About a third of the members who attended church that day became involved in some kind of community ministry. One leader with whom I spoke told me: "Most people want to do good, but they have to be led." Churches with a compassion ministry culture have leaders who lead their people in this direction.

   Fellowship Bible Church, in North Plano, Texas, has found that the most effective means of developing a culture of compassion ministry is to design it into their small group experiences. They rewrote their small groups manual and produced a DVD that explains their expectation that all of their small groups will have a ministry in the community. Pastor Glen Brechner says: "Outreach is always the hardest rock to push up the hill for any church, but we've learned that if you get your small groups involved it will not only make a difference in the community, it will develop deeper community within the small groups at your church."[5]

They often use terms such as compassion *or* serving the community *or* focused outward *to describe their church to others.* Language is a powerful indicator of values. One of the best ways of measuring the depth and breadth of a value in a group is to listen to the people in that group talk. The words they use will inevitably betray the group's values. In a culture of compassion ministry, the people talk about their ministries in the community, usually with pride. This need not be a prideful thing, but a defining thing–that is, something that defines the church. When your church members talk about the church to their neighbors, what do they say? What words do they use to describe the church? "Good"? "Welcoming"? "Warm"? "Good fellowship"? "Inspiring worship"? These are some of the words I hear most often. I seldom hear members speak about their church as "outwardly focused" or "compassionate" or "here for the community." Yet a church with a culture of compassion ministry *will* use these words and others like them.

The community knows them as people who care about the larger community. Few churches have any idea what people not associated with their church think of them. They have never gone to the trouble of discovering their reputations in their communities. On the one hand, this is understandable. This is not an easy thing to do. I know; I've tried. On the other hand, this is critical information for the church that desires to be connected with its community.

Compassion ministry influences their decision-making. Few things are as telling about a church as how the members make decisions. Inevitably, their values will come into play, especially in tough decisions. What sort of questions surface when the church faces difficult issues? Do they give priority to matters of security–whether the church will at least remain as strong as it is today–or are they willing to take risks for the sake of those outside the community? To what do they say, "No," and why? Have they made decisions that challenge them to move beyond their comfort zones for the sake of persons not in their fellowship?

When Hurricane Katrina hit New Orleans and Mississippi, hundreds of thousands of people were relocated all over the country. Some of them came as far as East Tennessee, where I live. Churches were asked quickly to take them in until a more permanent shelter arrangement could be put into place for the hurricane refugees. A large downtown congregation did just that. They took in fifty-seven people from Louisiana. They housed the refugees in their gym/fellowship hall. This meant that they would not have the use of this space for several weeks, no small inconvenience for the church. Sunday School classes had to relocate. Mid-week activities had to be rearranged. Most significantly, the contemporary worship service had to be moved to the traditional sanctuary.

You can see this was not an easy decision. Nevertheless, the church decided to provide a safe place for some of the Katrina victims. Reflecting on that decision, the pastor told me: "It was an Exodus moment for us in many ways. The church had said they wanted to be a missional church but up to that point had not experienced the kind of thing that could move us down that road. When we gathered for worship the Sunday morning when the evacuees were there, it was like a revival. We now point to that experience as a defining moment for our church." This is a church with a culture of compassion ministry.

People are attracted to them because of their compassion ministry. They draw other compassionate people to them. This is not the sort of thing that happens when a church does not have a comprehensive approach to compassion ministry, because hardly anyone outside the church knows about it, and, for that matter, many inside the church do not know about it.

As I travel the country presenting the Operation Inasmuch model of community ministry to congregational leaders and following up with them to learn of their experiences, I often hear that persons who have been on the fringe of the church, people who have attended but not yet made a decision to join the church, step over the line of membership as a result of the church giving compassion ministry priority. I hear about people who have been helped through an Operation Inasmuch who begin attending the church that helped them as a result. Possibly the most interesting story of this kind came to me out of a North Carolina church. When the church did their first Operation Inasmuch, an inactive member signed up to participate. He described himself as a "C & E Christian"–Christmas and Easter were the times he came to church. He learned of the opportunity to serve not through the normal means of church communication, but through the civic club of which he is a member. The church's Operation Inasmuch Coordinator came to the club and told them what the church was planning to do in a few weeks. The man signed up right away to participate in a wheelchair ramp project.

As the day of service approached, it was learned that this particular project needed to be done early and during the week as opposed to Saturday. Because this man is a professional with a full schedule, his project leader called to tell him that he was not expected to participate in building the wheelchair ramp since it was to be done on a Wednesday instead of Saturday. The man promptly cancelled all his appointments that day and was on hand to build the wheelchair ramp. Furthermore, when the Saturday of Operation Inasmuch rolled around, he was there, too, to help with another project. As impressive as this man's involvement was, it was even more impressive when he resumed regular attendance at worship as a result of participation in one experience of compassion ministry (or, to perhaps describe it more accurately, as a result of the *church's participation* in compassion ministry, resulting in his new perception of the church's direction and ministry). A church with a culture of compassion ministry attracts other compassion-minded people to it, or, as in this case, reclaims inactive members with the opportunity to serve.

A Tale of Two Churches

Let's take a look at a couple of churches with this culture at work. Trinity Baptist Church, Raleigh, North Carolina, and Mars Hill Baptist Church, Mars Hill, North Carolina, have experienced a transition in culture away from traditional structures toward a heavy investment in their communities. The leaders of both churches describe them as very different than they were ten years ago. They serve as models for any congregation that has a vision for becoming truly externally focused.

I acknowledge the limits of these model churches in that they are both Baptist and from the same state. However, their contexts are very different—one being urban and the other almost rural. They share one similarity. Both churches have made heavy use of Operation Inasmuch as a means to connect with their communities and redirect their energy outward.

Trinity Baptist Church

Trinity Baptist Church is a fifty-one-year-old Southern Baptist congregation in North Raleigh, North Carolina. As the city has grown, so has the church. North Raleigh has exploded with growth in the last couple of decades. Trinity is a church of about 2,500 members with an average weekend attendance of about 900. The staff estimates that as many as half of the active congregation is involved in eight to ten ongoing compassion ministries throughout the year. These ministries include:

- *Operation Inasmuch, twice a year:* Over 250 people involved in about three dozen projects throughout the community
- *Wake Interfaith Hospitality Network:* hosting several homeless families in church facilities four times a year, providing meals and transportation to and from school and work
- *World Changers:* Providing lunches to groups of teenagers in South Raleigh who give a week of their time to rehab inadequate housing for people in need
- *Operation Christmas Child Collection Center:* receive Operation Christmas Child shoe boxes from churches throughout North Raleigh and deliver them to a central distribution point elsewhere in the state
- *ESL Classes:* English as a Second Language for non-English speaking persons in the community
- *Jobs for Life Ministry:* a ministry of instruction and mentoring providing job readiness and character-building for unemployed and under-employed persons
- *North Raleigh Ministries:* A shared ministry with seven neighboring churches to provide emergency assistance and benevolent help to persons in need four days a week

When people ask the pastoral staff and lay leaders about Trinity's culture of compassion ministry, they say: "Compassion ministry is now seen as part of what it means to do church." They describe an atmosphere in which church members are more aware of their community. They have developed an accepting attitude toward the community. As an example, a Sunday School class became aware recently of a French family who settled in North Raleigh and needed a lot of help in becoming acclimated to their new community. The class immediately "adopted" the family and will assist them in their transition.

In recent years Trinity has developed a reputation in North Raleigh as a caring church. Examples are their serving as a collection center for the popular Operation Christmas Child. Another example is the establishment of North Raleigh Ministries (NRM). After years of conducting Operation Inasmuch, the church wanted to take the next step in meeting needs other than these one-day efforts. They led in the establishment of NRM and invited several churches in their area to come alongside them in providing emergency help for families. NRM began in 2004 and serves more than three thousand people each year. It is composed of a crisis center, thrift store, and food pantry. Leaders stress that the thrift store is one of the most popular places to shop in that all of the churches who provide clothing and household items for sale there tend to be affluent and, therefore, the items in the store are of high quality. The thrift store provides a significant portion of the funding for NRM, but Trinity has developed some creative funding approaches. When the church celebrates communion every other month, a special offering for NRM is received. Area restaurants offer special days in which 15 percent of church members' tab is given to the ministry.

Trinity's leaders have noticed a significant difference in how receptive the congregation is now to these types of ministries. For example, several years ago it was proposed that they provide lunches for teenagers ministering through World Changers in an economically depressed section of Raleigh. There was a fair amount of resistance to that proposition because of the perceived dangers. Now, they thoroughly embrace this ministry. As church leaders have proposed new compassion initiatives, such as the Interfaith Hospitality Network or the Jobs for Life Ministry, the church as taken them on almost without questions.

This is one of the more important indicators of a compassion ministry culture—that it is *expected* that the church will mobilize around this type of ministry. The questions that surface in the consideration of a new ministry idea are not *whether* the church should do it, but *how*? An even stronger indicator is the source of ministry ideas. Trinity has reached the point at which ways to minister to people in need are coming from the congregation rather than the professional staff. Jobs for Life Ministry is a good example. A member learned of the ministry, brought it to the attention of the leadership, said, "This is something we ought to be involved in," and is providing leadership for its implementation.

Not surprisingly, when asked how Trinity developed a culture of compassion ministry, members say it began with leadership. When the senior pastor and associate pastor came to the church a few years ago, they were vocal about their passion for missions. They talked about it and led mission trips. Then they came back and talked about their experiences. All this served to inspire interest and willingness to be more involved by members. Another key was the staff's ability to identify local needs and discover persons in the church who were passionate about serving and empowering them to devote their energies in that direction. As people come into the church, they are quickly shown opportunities to serve in compassion ministries and encouraged along the way. They do not have to "prove" themselves during a waiting period, but are trusted to jump in with both feet.

Culture shift is glacial—imperceptibly slow but changing everything. It's no different for churches. I asked Senior Pastor Jeff Roberts when he realized Trinity had made a culture shift toward compassion ministry. Here is what he said:

> I realized our church's culture had shifted when I reflected on three important decisions we made at about the same time. The first was not merely to respond once to the rebuilding efforts for the hurricane-devastated city of Gulfport, Mississippi, but also to make a year-long commitment to go back there once a month, leaving our disaster relief trailer on sight [sic] so others could make use of the materials. The second was the decision to allow homeless families live in our church facilities for a week at a time through the WHIN program. The last decision was the biggest step of faith—to rent a large space in a shopping center for North Raleigh Ministries. Each of these required faith [and] a willingness to partner with other churches and others. We have been called to have compassion for people in our community and in other

places. We have been teaching our congregation that being on mission must begin at home and expand to other parts of the world. In these three decisions and the consequent volunteer involvement, it occurred to me that our church was practicing what we were preaching.[6]

Mars Hill Baptist Church

Mars Hill Baptist Church is the leading congregation in the sleepy town of Mars Hill, located about twenty miles north of Asheville, North Carolina. It is a typical mountain community, with the exception of being home for Mars Hill College, a four-year Baptist college. The church campus is adjacent to the college. Attendance fluctuates with the seasons but averages between 200 and 250 people a weekend. Dr. Tommy Justus, the senior pastor, has served the church for twelve years. Over the years Mars Hill's church life has been dominated by college affairs. The fact that their sanctuary is way too large for the congregation is due to the fact that the church built a worship center that would accommodate the entire student body of Mars Hill College in a day when the students were required to attend chapel. Now the school has its own auditorium and the church has focused their outreach toward the larger community of Madison County.

The culture shift at Mars Hill began with the congregation opening their facilities to groups in the community. With the pastor's encouragement, they opened their doors to sports teams and other ministries such as a Pastoral Counseling Center and Advent Spirituality Center, both of which maintain offices in the church buildings. Mars Hill also hosts the Manna Outpost, a community food pantry. Over the years the attitude of the congregation shifted from, "These are *our facilities,*" to, "How can we use what God has provided here for others?"

Having been a youth pastor prior to coming to Mars Hill, it was natural for Justus to lead the congregation to serve the community through the teenagers. At his initiative, they began Operation Santa, in which school counselors helped them identify people in need and they provided Christmas for thirty to forty families in the larger community. The teens learned the true spirit of Christian service in this project in that they were careful to bring gifts to the families when the children were away from home so the parents could share with their children as if they, the parents, had provided them, hence the name Operation *Santa*. The adults who run this project now were teenagers when it began a dozen years ago.

In the late 1990s, Mars Hill began doing Operation Inasmuch. It became another ministry that advanced the culture shift for the church. It has now morphed into an ongoing ministry rather than a one-day, twice-a-year affair, as it began. Now, the needs of families in the community are regularly shared with the congregation and people step up to meet the needs. "The church has become a broker for compassion ministry in Madison County," says one lay leader. "One of the reasons for this," he continues, "is that we don't just go into a home one time and walk away without ever having additional contact with them. We build a relationship with them. When they have other needs, such as an illness, we put them on our prayer list and the church members pray for them. People around the church ask about these families as if they are members here."

There is little question about what the larger community thinks of the church. In a recent study, the church interviewed government, college, business, and other community leaders to ascertain their perceptions of the church. When asked about the church's most significant contributions to the community, they answered: Mars Hill Baptist Church is the center of the community life, the "in" church, and the center of activity; it gives aid to people in need, brings the community together, reaches out to the community, and is a "service church." The Home Health office and Mental Health Agency refer people to the church regularly. Elected officials refer people with needs to the church. Clearly, Mars Hill has earned the reputation as a caring, serving congregation.

Events become stories, which in turn fuel change. Mars Hill has several such stories. One is about Rodney, a teenager with a reputation for being a troublemaker. When he was younger, he was banned from riding the bus to school because of his behavior. His two brothers were also banned. To say Rodney was not popular at school would be a gross understatement. Then Rodney was in a serious automobile accident and he was paralyzed from the waist down. The school tried to raise money to help with his medical bills, but, because of his reputation, there wasn't much response.

When Mars Hill Baptist leaders proposed building a wheelchair ramp for Rodney's home, some of the youth at the church said: "We shouldn't be helping this guy." But they built the ramp anyhow. Later, they came back and installed a handicapped bathroom for Rodney. They replaced the wood stove, which furnished heat for the home in the cold mountain winters. They painted the interior of his home. Some of the church members gave him a dog. The result is Rodney is a changed young man. His attitude, once sour and acerbic, is softer and more accepting. His brothers have changed, too. They have worked on some of the projects when the church has served other families and are planning to continue. Rodney is not yet a believer, but he has learned about God's love, not through religious tracts, but through the lives of his Christian neighbors who live a lifestyle of compassion ministry. This is one of many ongoing stories that continue to shift the Mars Hill culture toward compassion ministry.

This shift is evident in how some of the members have begun to think. They are looking for new ways the church can serve the community. For example, one member who is a developer and who has purchased a large parcel of prime mountain land is planning to set aside some of the land and build a dormlike facility to house some of the people who come to Madison County every summer to work with the Madison County Housing Coalition. Another plants an acre of potatoes each year and gives the potatoes to lower-income families. As many as twenty church members help to dig the potatoes. Some of the families on the receiving end also help work the fields.

Finally, Mars Hill has attracted people from the area to attend their church because of their culture of compassion ministry. The Blevins family's first experience with Mars Hill was through Operation Inasmuch. Brandon, then sixteen years old, began attending the church with friends. In his first Sunday at Mars Hill, he learned of the church's plans to help people in their community on a Saturday of hands-on compassion ministry. It sounded like fun to him, so he signed up. Then he invited his family to work with him and his friends in building a wheelchair ramp for a disabled family. When the opportunity to serve came around again, the Blevinses were there again. Russ, the father, says: "We decided that we were working with Mars Hill Baptist and maybe we should worship with them, too." A short time later they began attending the church and joined. The entire Blevins family is now among those who sport a lifestyle of compassion ministry through the life of Mars Hill Baptist.

Lessons Learned

These stories are meant to encourage and inspire. They can also teach us how to lead a church to make a shift in their default thinking toward compassion ministry. Let's look at some of the lessons learned here about developing a culture for compassion ministry in a church.

Leadership is indispensable. Did you notice that both congregations began their journey toward a new culture when new leaders came on board? Lay leaders at Trinity pointed to leadership (they were talking about the pastoral team) as the key to their culture shift. Their pastors talked about compassion ministry *and led by example.* The congregation learned of this priority by watching their leaders.

Preaching and teaching biblical compassion produces results. The church has an advantage in considering a cultural shift. We have the Bible—our sole authority for all we do as church. We take all of our direction from the Scriptures. When we talk about compassion from the Bible, our people listen. They may not respond as quickly as we think they should, but that doesn't mean they don't hear. It just takes a while for some seeds to germinate. If we believe, "God's word does not return to us void" (see Isa. 55:11), then we always have the Word in our toolbox for the purpose of reshaping the church's culture. Some of the Scripture passages that speak clearly about the priority of compassion ministry are:

Deuteronomy 10:18–19
Deuteronomy 14:28–29a
Deuteronomy 24:19–22
Micah 6:8
Luke 4:16–19
Matthew 25:31ff
Luke 10:25–37
Ephesians 2:8–10

Offer opportunities for compassion ministry. In both Trinity and Mars Hill, one-day projects and other short-term opportunities to serve people in need served as catalysts for their culture shift. As church folk became personally involved in these ministries, God began working on them, reshaping their thinking and opening them to other possibilities. One thing led to another, so that over time the shift had taken place. In the cases of Trinity and Mars Hill, Operation Inasmuch served that purpose, but there are other ministries that can accomplish the same thing, as discussed in chapter 6.

Facilitate reflection on experiences with compassion ministry. Most people will talk about their experiences, especially those they enjoy. What I am suggesting here is that the church be intentional in connecting the biblical concepts and instructions about compassion ministry to persons' actual experiences with it. People do not automatically make these connections, but when it happens, it is a powerful force for personal change–bringing biblical truth together with personal experience.

Becoming

None of the leaders of the Trinity or Mars Hill churches say their church has arrived. They admit that significant portions of their members still are not as involved in compassion ministry as they would like, but they are pleased and honest about their progress. One of them said with emotion: "I am overwhelmed by how far we've come." Whereas others reading about Trinity and Mars Hill might share their leaders' amazement at their progress toward an authentic compassion ministry culture, they are unwilling to announce that they have arrived. They are on a journey, but they have not yet arrived. They are becoming.

And isn't that the way it is in the Kingdom? None of us will "arrive" this side of heaven. As long as there are people who need to be served and ministered to, as long as there are church folk who are inwardly focused either because of selfishness or ignorance, and as long as institutional matters pressure the church to wander away from Jesus' calling of her, there will be work to do and progress yet to be made in this journey.

Notes

[1]Robert Lewis and Wayne Cordeiro, *Culture Shift: Transforming Your Church from the Inside Out* (San Francisco: Jossey-Bass, 2005), 3.

[2]Ibid., 49–50.

[3]Rick Rusaw and Eric Swanson, *Externally Focused Churches* (Loveland, Colo.: Group Publishing, 2004), 24–29 .

[4]Ibid., 15–16.

[5]Glen Brechner, as quoted in Krista Petty, "Externally Focused Small Groups," 3, posted on the Leadership Network Web site, www.leadnet.org.

[6]Jeff Roberts, e-mail dated September 4, 2007.